PILLAGE OF HOPE

PILLAGE OF HOPE

A Family History from the Trail of Tears, Slavery, Segregation, the 1921 Race Massacre and Beyond

MEMOIR BY DON ROSS

Acknowledgments

I want to thank the following individuals for their commitment to breathing life into this memoir. They helped immensely with everything from editing, consulting, formatting, and providing impactful input:

Jennifer Morales, Ellen Bravo, Dan Hardy, Jack Norman, Larry Miller, and Shane Amaya.

Thank you for your time and commitment in making this book a reality.

Copyright © 2021 by Edward Ross

All rights reserved

Printed and bound in the United States

Contents

	Foreword	*vii*
01	Big Mama Knew White Folk	11
02	My Family on the Trail of Tears	29
03	Oklahoma: A Black Blessing?	37
04	Bloodline: Thicker Than Water	41
05	Black Wall Street's Dark Side	49
06	Tale of a Race War	57
07	Outgunned and Outlawed	63
08	Blacks Instigate Riot?	79
09	The 60's	91
10	Black Wall Street Forgotten	105
11	A Black Quota	123
12	Riot Scars	135
13	Riot Impact	143
14	Reparations Doomed	149
15	Blacks Salute Confederacy	165
16	Memorial Without Eulogy	173
	Epilogue	*179*
	Recommendations	*183*
	Resources	*185*

Foreword

By Edward Ross and Larry Miller

For decades, the 1921 massacre of Black men, women and children in Greenwood, Oklahoma, and the destruction of the town's Black Wall Street were unknown to most people in the United States. One of the people credited with bringing the matter to light, Don Ross, has written an extraordinary memoir that gives readers a window into what happened in his community. The book, completed in 2014, describes the backstory to the 1921 attack, the massacre itself, the efforts to block rebuilding, the long years of silence, and Ross's efforts to break that silence, win reparations and other steps toward justice for Tulsa's Black community. In the six years since it was first written, the memoir has become even more meaningful given national attention to the upcoming centennial of the massacre, the growing influence of Black Lives Matter and the debates about racial injustice.

Don Ross, a civil rights organizer, journalist and state legislator, devoted his life to rectifying what happened in 1921. He first wrote about the massacre in a local publication in 1971. Later he was elected to the Oklahoma state assembly, where he introduced legislation to create a commission on the massacre, eventually leading to a call for reparations. He helped secure funding for the Greenwood Cultural Center, a prominent institution that combines history, arts and leadership education. A 1999 interview on *60 Minutes* and a feature article that year in *The New York Times Magazine* depicted Don Ross as "the man who brought the riot back to life."

This memoir combines Ross's personal and family history with the history of Oklahoma and this nation founded through the blood, sweat and tears of African Americans. His reflections on the arrival of his ancestors to Oklahoma — some as slaves walking the Trail of Tears, others freedmen and women, and some of mixed heritage — sheds light on the complexity of this emerging territory. Ross documents the inevitable path from a state founded in white supremacy and violence to the mass lynching Greenwood experienced on May 31, 1921.

In the book, Ross explains the complex relationship between African Americans, Native Americans and whites in the formation of Oklahoma. He interweaves his family's history with the state's history, relying on extensive research of tribal records, family records, court records and oral history, along with other primary documents and historical manuscripts. As a student and disciple of the historian John Hope Franklin, Ross links this story to African American experience nationwide—a story of oppression, resistance, ingenuity and resilience.

Ross first learned about the Tulsa massacre from a teacher in high school when he was 15 years old. Young Ross at first insisted such an attack could not have taken place, and then came to realize his family, neighbors, and the members of his church were all aware of what happened to their community some 35 years earlier. "The riot would influence my passion for civil rights and my advocacy against the war in Vietnam," he writes. "It led me on the road to becoming a journalist, an Oklahoma lawmaker, and to an unshakable empathy for poor and disenfranchised people struggling up the mountain top."

Ross's early adulthood included a stint in the army, involvement in CORE (the Congress of Racial Equality), and an interest in joining mainstream America. But this path was interrupted in 1966 by two white VISTA volunteers who, aghast at hearing stories from elders in the community about an assault never taught in American schools, pestered Ross to do something to bring the story to light. Ross describes the first response he received from community leaders: "Blacks want to forget the riot and whites may react with hostility to any discussions of it." Still, he was determined to find a way.

In 1982, Ross was elected to the Oklahoma state assembly,

representing Tulsa's North Side. There he was able to lead a successful fight, along with State Senator Maxine Horner, for funding to create the Greenwood Cultural Center, in honor of Black Wall Street and the resistance of the Black community. He also pursued a fight for reparations in the wake of national attention on Oklahoma after the 1995 attack on the federal building in Oklahoma City. That same year, the Florida legislature awarded individual payments to survivors of the 1923 Rosewood massacre, setting an important precedent. Ross introduced legislation that created the 1997 Oklahoma Commission to Study the Tulsa Race Riot. In his memoir, he deconstructs the work of the commission and the city and state politics that doomed reparations at that time.

Among his achievements was decommissioning the Confederate flag being flown in the Oklahoma statehouse—a policy reversed after he left the assembly in 2002.

The memoir ends with Don Ross detailing his relationship with survivors of the 1921 massacre and the lawsuits they undertook. He makes a powerful case for reparations. Harvard Professor Charles Ogletree Jr. has called Tulsa "ground zero" in the reparations discussion. It is our hope that this memoir will help build momentum for long-overdue justice to be served.

For most of Don Ross's life, the event that started on May 31, 1921, was called a "riot." Throughout the memoir, he uses that term. After Ross completed this memoir, the community agreed to call that day what it truly was: a massacre, a mass lynching.

Thanks to significant local and national attention over the last few years, the investigation into what happened in Greenwood was reopened, leading to the discovery of mass graves. Numerous community art and education initiatives have encouraged reflection about the history of Greenwood and beyond. Curriculum about Black Wall Street and the 1921 massacre is being taught in Tulsa Public Schools. Unlike the silence Don Ross experienced, the public can now find books (fiction and nonfiction), videos, curricula and presentations describing this history. The HBO series *Watchmen* depicted the massacre, leading millions of viewers to seek more information about the truth of what happened.

Standing in the heart of what's known as "deep Greenwood," the Greenwood Cultural Center helped prepare for this outpouring of work. The Center serves as testimony to Oklahoma's Black workers, farmers, pioneers, trailblazers, entrepreneurs and all of the citizens who made up the historic Black Wall Street community and the many surrounding Black townships. Its mission remains to bring Greenwood's history to life in order to promote and preserve African-American culture and heritage.

The Center fulfills that mission with a mix of historical displays, lectures and walk-through presentations. The Summer Arts Program gives children the opportunity to explore various forms of art, music, creative writing, dance, theater and more with respected community educators such as pottery artist Yusuf Etudaiye and trumpeter D.G. Rozay-El.

Other offerings for young people include leadership development programs for middle-school girls through the Women of Tomorrow initiative, and afterschool programs in Tulsa Public Schools. In addition, the Center now hosts the Children's Defense Fund Freedom Schools Program.

Like the survivors of the 1921 massacre, Don Ross's wish is for the world never to forget what happened and to help repair the damage. The Greenwood Cultural Center he helped birth and this memoir, are powerful means to keep that solemn promise.

1
Big Mama Knew White Folk

He who controls the land controls the legacy and the history that is cultivated there.
　　　　　　　　　　　Maxine Horner, retired Oklahoma State Senator

MY GRANDMOTHER'S FAMILY arrived in Indian Territory with the Creek Indians. Some were slaves. Others were Freedmen and tribal members. My slave ancestors, William and Affie Bruner, were ultimately freed before the Civil War by their owners, and my grandmother eventually prospered. But in 1921, she lost everything to the infamous events that came to be known as the Tulsa Race Riot. Over the course of two days, white Oklahomans attacked the Greenwood section of Tulsa—then the nation's most prosperous Black community—burning or bombing businesses and homes, and injuring or imprisoning thousands. Before the September 11, 2001, attack on New York's World Trade Center, the 1921 Tulsa race war was called the worst act of terrorism on U.S. soil since the Civil War. As many as 300 persons may have been murdered in the riot.

The Tulsa riot was hidden from history for more than 75 years in a nearly complete conspiracy of silence. Only later did I learn how directly it had affected my family.

This is the story of how their community developed, the fierce backlash to their prosperity and independence, the aftermath of that 1921 massacre, and my role in fighting to remember and repair what our community lost, and to honor its resilience.

MY ANCESTORS WERE AMONG the thousands of slaves, Freedmen, and Black tribal members who were herded from the South to what is now Oklahoma, swept up in the United States' "Indian removal" project of the 1830s. The Native Americans of Florida, Georgia, Mississippi, and Alabama were viewed as barriers to whites' future development of these lands. My ancestors endured struggles and suffering on the long, frigid Trail of Tears as they made the trek alongside what was known as the Five Civilized Tribes. The Cherokee, Chickasaw, Choctaw, Creek, and Seminole were called "civilized" for adopting the ways of whites, including slavery. With rifles and bayonets, the five tribes and their Black companion travelers were forcibly removed from ancestral lands in the South to what was then called Indian Territory.

There were five separate, painful treks made by the Cherokee, Chickasaw, Choctaw, Creek, and Seminole, their 7,000 Black slaves, Freedmen and Black tribal members. Nearly 50,000 members of the Five Civilized Tribes were removed and made subjects of the government's "benevolence" in the Indian Territory's poverty-stricken concentration camps. Up to 10,000 died in-route.

The shared hardships on the Trail of Tears didn't breed comradery between Native Americans and Blacks. The slave master's relationship was well-defined, and Indians saw slaves as property and slave ownership remained a treasured entitlement.

Historical records have my family settled in "The Territory" in 1830. The first recorded death in the family, my great-great-great-grandfather Jacob Grayson, died as a slave during the Civil War.

The tribes had sided with the Confederacy. After the Civil War ended, the United States negotiated new treaties with each of the five southern Indian nations. Ratified in 1866, the treaties provided for the abolition of slavery and the extension of citizenship, including land rights, to the freed slaves. Through the rest of the century, Blacks in the nations struggled to secure their citizenship and land rights. When the five nations were dissolved under the Curtis Act (1898), both Blacks and Indians were compelled to accept land allotments and become legal residents of the state of Oklahoma. One hundred and sixty acres were allotted to Black Freedmen, tribal members and their descendants.

My grandmother's family arrived in Indian Territory with the Creek Indians. Some were slaves. Others were Freedmen and tribal members. My slave ancestors, William and Affie Bruner, were ultimately freed before the Civil War by their owners. Their family and others were granted a 160-acre allotment of Creek Tribal land at the close of the Civil War. My grandmother, Mary Ann Jones, and her brother shared that land.

Oklahoma Blacks are the progeny of injustices that have framed the state's racial psyche. And yet, Black pioneers in the territory before and after statehood made a way out of no way. "Survival" was their temporary metaphor for "emancipation." My family and other Blacks of early Oklahoma sighted freedom and fought the oppression. They were neither suffocated by the hardships of slavery from Indians or the riot, nor were they crushed from the subjugation of segregation.

Oklahoma Blacks are unique and different from their racial kin held in bondage in the Deep South. Slavery was not as harsh among the Indians. Some Blacks were tribal leaders and they had participated in the inhumanity. That legacy remains even today. I have relatives who are listed on the Indian rolls as Creek, others as Freedmen, and some who are not listed on the rolls at all.

This history, the treachery and forked tongues, delineated my early childhood and my life. I was born in Tulsa 20 years after the Black community was destroyed. When I finally learned about the race riot, its cruelty and violence contradicted my view of white people. As a youngster I was told by old folks that "peckerwoods," the derogatory description for whites by Blacks, could be mean, but most were not as ornery and dangerous as in the days of slavery. However, it was youthful experiences in Vinita, Oklahoma, some 60 miles north of Tulsa, that set my first views on race. In the late 1930s, Big Mama (my grandmother Mary) married Tommy Bean, a Black Vinita Cherokee tribal member, and she moved to Vinita to live with her new husband. On the Trail of Tears, his family had come to Oklahoma with the Cherokees, while her relatives traveled with the Creeks. Tommy Bean's people were tribal members, while Big Mama's folks were a mix of slaves, Freedmen and tribal members.

When I was three years old, my mama and my dad were in search of work. My uncle urged them to move to Kansas City, Missouri, from Tulsa, where our family had lived for generations. Hard times followed them. There were no jobs and ultimately no marriage.

Mama was nineteen with three small boys when they divorced. Big Mama urged my mother to relocate to Vinita and together they would make ends meet. Big Mama's stories and her rationales for racism would teach me plenty about the limitations facing Blacks in a white world. Quietly, she considered herself more Creek Indian than Black.

We moved from Kansas City to Vinita in 1945. I was six years old. Arriving at the Vinita train station from Kansas City after the break-up is among my earliest memories. I had to "use it." Mama said, "Wait 'til you get home." Only after the mule-drawn wagon arrived at the four-room shack, trimmed in yellow imitation brick siding, was I ushered through the cold winter's air to the outhouse far behind it.

After I "used it," I scrubbed my behind with corn cobs piled in a nearby crate and dropped them into the deep hole in the ground. I wondered why I couldn't have used the facility in the train station, maybe even had real newspaper to clean up.

I saw my dad only once after we moved, 21 years later, in a coffin during his funeral in Oakland, California. He had two other families with several children. I have only met my sister Tonya and brother Ronald. The day my dad was buried closed a lonely chapter in my life, a festering wound still aching long after he deserted me and my brothers.

Later, my stepfather, Floyd Vann, would stand in his place—like a soldier volunteering for an uncertain and thankless duty. Floyd's ancestors had also been subjected to the long march to Indian Territory on the Trail of Tears and the Vanns were among the first settlers in Vinita. Big Mama's husband, Tommy Bean, was Floyd's great uncle. Mama's man was good, decent, and caring. Still, I could never call him "Pop" as my brothers did. There was something artificial, incomplete, and unofficial about that. I called him by his first name, Floyd. My father had left a large gap in my feelings and Floyd never breached the divide. Deep down in my soul I think I blamed Mama for not holding on to my real Pop, maybe the only man who could've made me feel whole and complete. Floyd held my respect and my genuine love, but he just wasn't Pop.

Mama became a cook at Scotty's Café and worked long hours. My two brothers and I were under the care of Big Mama. I think we brought a bit of happiness and an occasional smile to her otherwise drab existence.

Big Mama was a near look-alike of the Black woman whose face appeared on boxes of a brand of pancake mix—an Aunt Jemima replica without the grin. There were age lines tattooed on her round, cocoa-brown face, signs of her nearly 50 years. A girdle line showed through the print dress. Her light-brown stockings were coiled below her knees. She never was without a white apron and checkered scarf over her head.

Big Mama shifted her heavy frame from one leg to the other as she wobbled through the house or in the yard, fed chickens, churned butter, slopped hogs, stooped to pull potatoes from the large garden and carried water from the well in the backyard. Her long, braided hair was tied into a knot and stuffed under the scarf. As she worked—cooking, washing, ironing and humming gospel songs—she paused only to threaten the noisy grandchildren as the youngsters attempted to dismantle the leaning house. During the rains, several rusty pails caught the dripping water.

Vinita was wonderful. In Kansas City, kids were imprisoned in small apartments. In Vinita, everybody lived in a house. Children were scolded and told to "get out yonder and play" in the acres of vacant pasture. During games, I was always the proud Indian, as my grandma insisted she was. I was never modest in explaining my Indian pedigree to playmates. My friend Peewee rejected the notion: "You's a nigger." His insult may have gained the laughter, but I won the fight.

On Saturdays, neighborhood youngsters shuffled off to the movies to cheer for Roy Rogers. Black kids could not ride with Gene Autry. The singing cowboy played at the Aztec Theater where Blacks were banned. They herded us into the balcony of the Center Theater where Roy Rogers was king of the cowboys. From those days I associate Autry with injustice and Rogers as a bit kinder.

The movies and Big Mama's proud Indian connection framed my view of the world outside Vinita. When John Wayne was surrounded by our braves, I wanted the "Great Spirits" to send us help. Help never came. It was back to the reservation for my people. I couldn't understand why people were separated at the movies and on the Indian reservations. There were plenty of empty seats downstairs and room for the Indians where the buffaloes roamed. I asked my grandmother. Big Mama described the yokes of segregation in terms of chores. Her second husband, Tommy Bean, had this Jersey cow. Each morning he took the cow to the bottom land for grazing. He tied a long rope to a stake driven into the ground, with the other end wrapped around the animal's neck. The cow ate the grass in the circle allowed by the leash. The rope established where the cow could go. Segregation was a rope that held colored folks in place. If the cow tried to move outside the circle, the rope yanked the animal back in his place. Like the Jersey cow, colored people were only allowed to graze within the circle allowed by the rope. I wondered why we were treated like cows with a little circle and white people had the whole pasture. She said, "That's the law." For her there were two rules Black folks were required to follow: What they could do and what they could not do. Big Mama called the laws "a cross colored folks had to bear." Big Mama knew white folks well.

I often overheard adults speak of a flashing neon sign in the window of the Grand Cafe. One afternoon, after riding with Roy Rogers, I walked from the movie to the cafe and saw the sign. Later I asked Big Mama: "What is nigger fried chicken?" She described it as golden brown and well-seasoned. That was the way I liked my chicken wings then and now.

Chicken was our main staple at dinner on Sundays. It was big fun watching Big Mama wring the hens' necks, leaving them hopping wildly, then dump them into the large black kettle filled with scalding hot water so she could pull their feathers. It was rare when the kids got one of the good pieces, particularly the drumstick. Kids ate the back, neck, liver, gizzard and even the tough yellow clawed feet. Occasionally the wings were left for us. Only the chicken's guts were discarded.

Big Mama Knew White Folk

On other weekends, the neighborhood gang slipped onto the grounds of the all-white Riverside School to ride the swings, seesaws and carousels. The cops would come and chase us away, sometimes escorting us home. The ride in the police car was part terror, but mostly fun. We were told "trespassing is against the law." There was fussing from our folks—"y'all stay off dem white folks' stuff." On other occasions when we were again trespassing, the police sped past with red lights flashing. Evidently, we were not the only crooks thereabouts.

Years later I talked to my friend and Tulsa neighbor, Vernon Glenn. He was Vinita's police chief when I was young. Glen said he learned about our harassment years later when the boys gathered and retold old stories. "They were having their redneck fun," Glen asserted. He confirmed that we were not violating segregation laws. The former chief said our folks knew if they complained, later they could be hauled to jail on trumped-up charges. "That happened," he said. "It happened a lot."

I never heard of police brutality in Vinita, however arresting Blacks on minor or questionable charges was routine. For some, fines were considered a Black tax. We were taught to say only two things to policemen: "Yes, sah," and "No, sah." There were at least three basic rules kids were taught early: Move off the sidewalks when approaching whites. Never look a white woman in the eye. Take off your hat when speaking with whites. One-time, Big Mama's coaching on how to talk to whites worked. I went into Clyde's Store with a nickel to buy a cup of ice cream. Clyde was talking with a white customer who had laid a quarter on the counter to pay for tobacco. Clyde told him to wait until he finished with me.

"Whatcha want? Ice cream?"

"Yes, sah."

He picked up the man's quarter and gave me 20 cents in change. As I was leaving, the customer was complaining that he had paid a quarter for the tobacco. "I put it right there, pointing at the counter. "Maybe the nigger got it," he suggested.

"Come here, boy. Did you pick up his money?" Clyde asked.

"No, sah."

17

Clyde said maybe he had put it in the cash register. "That's Mary's grandson. He ain't gonna lie to me." And I had not.

Twenty years later I returned to Clyde's Store, told him the story, and attempted to return the 20 cents in change he had given me.

"That story is worth money." He insisted that I take a pint of ice cream. "On the house this time," and he laughed.

In Vinita, Blacks were as western and as cowboy as whites. Black cowboys were scouts for the military and Indian tribes. They worked on ranches, drove cattle down the Chisholm Trail and after the Civil War gained fame and respect as Buffalo Soldiers.

A Black man, Bill Pickett, perfected the rodeo entertainment called bulldogging: the art of wrestling a steer to ground. Unfortunately, Black cowboys never galloped through our history books, or appeared in westerns on the screens of the Aztec or Center Theaters. The first Black I saw in a western movie was former Los Angeles Rams football star, Woody Strodes—and he played an Indian. There were remnants of the old west among Black men in Vinita. They walked with a swagger and dressed as wranglers with wide-brimmed Stetson hats, shined boots, and Levi's jeans with large silver belt buckles. They even "yeehawd" like white folks.

Regardless of race, the people of Vinita looked forward to the annual western roundup. The Will Rogers Memorial Rodeo is the only such cowboy show sanctioned by the Oklahoma humorist. Black youngsters and some adults avoided paying admission by slipping under the fence. Bleachers reserved for "coloreds only" were next to the holding pens and the foul odor of the livestock. Even Bill Pickett would be required to sit near the stench. Still, Blacks cheered when there was a good performance and laughed at the clowns.

After Labor Day, Black kids lined up to walk nearly two miles to Attucks School. We dutifully moved off the sidewalk when whites were approaching. White kids were chauffeured in yellow school buses. They laughed at us, shouted names, obscenities and offered "the finger."

Vinita Blacks have a rich history. In 1899 the Commissioner of Indian Affairs noted that Freedmen in the village were the most industrious and economical in the Territory "and are anxious that their children shall be educated." Before statehood, some Blacks attended Indian schools, but the strained relationship failed. Blacks opened private schools in their homes and churches. In 1900, a four-room wood-frame building was erected for Blacks. It was later torn down to develop a new school built with WPA funds. Pioneering Blacks proudly insisted it be named for Crispus Attucks, the Freedman-sailor who was the first to die during the Boston Massacre that triggered the Revolutionary War.

In 1946, I became a student at Attucks School, where learning was mandatory. Two grades were housed in each classroom, first through the twelfth. All students were taught music on toy instruments. Attucks elementary students even had a school band, albeit with toy instruments. Only the cymbals were real.

Once, the band was invited to perform at a Vinita School Board concert. We were dressed in white shirts and white britches with a handmade purple cloak draped across our shoulders. As we marched through the neighborhood, grown folk lined the sidewalks and looked from the porches, and clapped in cadence. The band would stop, play a tune, dance a jig, and move on, to the approving shouts from elders: "That's my baby! Do it—get down." The instruments may have been toys, but we had rhythm.

The Attucks band was ushered into the Vinita High School's gym, roped off from the white students who had real instruments. I wondered why. Another cross colored folks had to bear? Then our music teacher Miss Barbara Jean Kelly pointed toward me, I clashed the cymbals and it didn't matter. After we finished, the all-white audience stood and applauded. It felt good to meet with white folks' approval.

En route to school we passed "The Park." If the park for "coloreds" had a name then, nobody ever told me. During Juneteenth (the June 19th celebration of the Emancipation Proclamation), and other holidays, the community gathered at The Park in the cinder block building on the west corner of Second Street. The women cooked and the kids played games: pin the tail on the donkey, dunking for apples, and—out of sight of parents—hide and seek, where, after finding a girl, she could be kissed without threatening to tell her mama.

We watched and learned a butt-banging version of the square

dance. Outside, men drank homemade Choc (Choctaw) beer and corn whiskey and never tired of hearing half-drunk Hank Johnson's entertaining rendition of a 1950 Johnny Otis hit song. Hank sang in the voices of both Little Esther Phillips and Mel Walker:

Little Esther: Why don't you go out there and fight a great big black grizzly bear?

Mel Walker: Why don't you go?

Little Esther: I'm a lady.

Mel Walker: They got lady bears out there.

The large field at The Park was absent any playground equipment. It was furnished with wooden bleachers in various stages of disrepair, screened by a ragged fence behind a baseball diamond where large rocks served as bases. There, local athletes placed their skills against the barnstorming Kansas City Monarchs, the Indianapolis Clowns, and the other elites of the Negro Baseball League.

It is a Vinita legend that my Uncle John Henry stood down Satchel Paige's team from the pitcher's mound and afterwards was recruited by the Black baseball pros. His promising career ended with the bombing of Pearl Harbor. He returned from the war as a broken man, an alcoholic. Though Blacks were barred from all other playgrounds, whites came to challenge our ball players at The Park.

Every man on our team was convinced he would be discovered, join Jackie Robinson, and become the next of our race to star with the Brooklyn Dodgers. Any loss to "the crackers" (another offensive name for whites) was blamed on cheating. All the authority figures and referees were white. It was inconceivable that "the patties" (still another distasteful description for white) could win fairly.

After any game, the smell of barbecue lured baseball fans to a whitewashed hut across the street. The owner had been teased as a youngster that he was "so Black that he was blue" and so that was the name of the joint: "Blue's." Blue's tall white chef's hat stuck sideways from his head, on a neckless frame notably absent of proper diet or exercise.

Blue smeared his secret sauce across the ribs until each of the tables was served. From the jukebox, the boogie-woogie blues of Ruth Brown, B.B. King, Muddy Waters, Louis Jordan, Bobby "Blue"

Bland, "Big" Joe Turner, Count Basie, Ernie Fields, Dinah Washington, Roy Milton and others would moan their harmony of misery and dejected love as men and women circled the dance floor cheek to cheek.

Blue's was the only place in Vinita where social customs and the rigid rules of segregation were relaxed. Whites came, ate, mingled freely, and guzzled down Pabst Blue Ribbon beer without the burden of the cross colored folks had to bear. White men more than flirted with Black women and nobody seemed to notice.

On a September evening in 1948, I marched to the train station with Uncle John Henry and other uniformed Black World War II veterans to welcome President Harry S. Truman's whistle-stop campaign passing through Vinita. After World War II, Truman offered Blacks some hope for change when he ended segregation in the military.

I suspect every Black in town turned out for the man who had stood for their equality. Truman was the first American President to launch an assault on discrimination and lynching and the first president to speak to the NAACP Convention. I don't remember what the President said, but Blacks and whites eagerly shouted, "Give 'em hell, Harry!"

After President Truman's speech I joined the long line to use the lavatory. I then understood why Mama refused to allow me to use the toilet marked "colored." She wanted to protect me from two indignities: The facility was segregated and it stank. It was filthy and without corn cobs or newspaper to clean myself. Separate but equal toilets didn't mean the colored place had to be clean or sanitary. It was the law.

On the day President Truman's whistle-stop tour pulled into Vinita, NAACP lawyer Amos T. Hall, of Tulsa, filed a lawsuit against the racist election practice in Oklahoma that labeled African-American Justice of Peace candidates as "Negro" on the ballot. He won the case. Hall was one of the NAACP's trial attorneys who won two landmark Supreme Court cases that led to the integration of higher education in Oklahoma and the nation. In one of the cases, federal Judge Alfred P. Murrah ruled that G.W. McLaurin was entitled to secure a post-graduate education in the state. Hall later became my friend and mentor and Oklahoma's first Black judge. A federal building was named for Judge Murrah and later was bombed by Timothy McVeigh in 1995.

Back home, I was to learn that Big Mama had a dark side. Church was as certain as Saturday night's bath—a once-a-week ritual in which the three boys bathed in the same tub of water that Big Mama packed from the backyard well.

One Sunday, my brothers, Toote and Snooky, and I were sniffling a bit. She filled each of us with Hadacol, a reputed cure for everything from snakebites to measles and other medicinal reasons when corn whiskey was unavailable. She wrapped around our necks a plug of an old Indian remedy, the God-awful smelling asafetida.

Before she left for church, she rolled the leftover breakfast oatmeal into cookies and pulled them from the oven. The smell of the cookies brought the devil out in me. But I promised Jesus I would eat just one. I leaned a chair against the mahogany china cabinet filled with plates, dishes, and glasses given to her by a rich white radio preacher for whom she had worked. The fine china was only used when the preacher or white folks came calling. As I reached for the top where the cookies were cooling, I slipped and pulled the cabinet to the floor. Amidst the broken glass, I meant to nibble down just one, but maybe even Jesus wouldn't miss a second. I took a third back with me to the couch where she had ordered me to nap. I have never understood why sin is so enjoyable. I squeezed my eyes shut and tried to sleep, but the tick-tocks from the grandfather clock were just too loud.

Later I heard the door squeak open and slam. Pounding footsteps took her to a bedroom where she changed from her Sunday clothes to her apron and work clothes. She pulled a blanket over me, and then entered the kitchen. A shout: "Don, Toote, Snooky! Get in here!" The mahogany china cabinet was in splinters. Broken plates and glasses were scattered over the floor.

"Who did this?" she screamed, all the while looking me straight in the eyes. There was quiet. Big Mama hollered, "Who broke my stuff?"

In perfect harmony the three of us answered "Not me, Big Mama."

Then it happened—the most astonishing thing in the history of grandparenting. Big Mama said if somebody confessed, nobody would get a spanking. If they didn't, everybody would get the whipping.

Sounded like a deal to me. I answered, "I did it and I'm sorry." I was so proud of myself. I had told the truth like the Bible said and in doing so saved myself from sin and my brothers from a near-death experience. "God is good," I thought.

It never occurred to me that Big Mama's apparent mercy had disguised her cruelty. She stormed out the back door and in seconds returned with a lethal weapon, the mother of all tree limbs.

She beat me so heartlessly and for so long that the dogs began mimicking my howling from the backyard. Clearly, she would be charged with child abuse today. This was the first time I realized that even church-going old folks would lie.

When her drunken husband came home and saw the rubble he grabbed me and his razor strap. Armed with an iron frying pan, she backed him away from me. From then, it would never be good between him and my brothers and me.

Big Mama answered complaints from her grandchildren on her husband's harsh treatment by saying, "He don't like anybody. He's just mean."

We couldn't call him "Grandpa." "I ain't got no grandchillen," he told us. So, he became "Uncle Tommy."

Often Uncle Tommy would get smashed from corn whiskey and then there would be a loud, threatening fuss. When Uncle Tommy finally got on what Big Mama called "my last nerve," she abandoned her high, Christian morals and began hanky-panky with another man. After an argument, Uncle Tommy slapped her. She left with nothing but the clothes on her back and moved in with Jeff Irons.

From the day Big Mama left the house, the focus of the evening feud switched to Mama. I heard new words: "bitch," "slut," "whore," "Jezebel."

"That's why that nigger left your loose ass in Kansas City," he yelled at Mama. That hurt. Snooky would cry, then me, and finally tears flowed down the cheek of my stubborn brother Toote. Uncle Tommy ordered Mama and her "bad-ass brats" from his house. We were homeless in the cold of winter, and Mama was pregnant with my sister Pearly, Floyd Vann's child.

Floyd was Uncle Tommy's great-nephew. On a cold, snowy morning Floyd packed the kids and all our stuff into an old Packard held together by rust, with the road clearly visible through holes in the floorboards, and took us to his mother's house. His mother, "Miss Ethel," and Uncle John Henry were the only adults in the house I remember as being nice to us.

There were three generations living in the small two-bedroom house. Toote, Snooky and me slept on the floor of a covered porch where the cruel cold could be felt through the cracks in the walls. On very cold, snowy evenings, the thin blankets offered little defense against the cold. We bundled together and eased our shivering with body heat.

Meanwhile, on one of his drunken splurges, Uncle Tommy kicked in the front door of Jeff Irons' house and cut loose on my grandmother's lover with both barrels of a sawed-off shotgun. Jeff Irons was dead. Big Mama fled to Tulsa before the funeral.

In this small idyllic village with contagious poverty and infectious loyalties, everybody was either a relative of Uncle Tommy or Jeff Irons and took their respective family's side in the scandal. However, both sides blamed Big Mama, Mama, and us. That was the first time a Black had been killed in Vinita since the Civil War. Uncle Tommy sold his bottom land, hired Vinita's best white lawyer and never spent a day in jail.

Vinita was not fun after that. I fought on every corner. I bluffed the larger bullies: "I'll cut your head off and shove it in the toilet with the rest of the shit." Defensive humor became my trademark. I'm teased by those friends today that what I then called "winning a fight" was simply that I could take a punch.

After the winter, Mama and Floyd moved into a house on North Fourth Street. In all eyes but God, the law and the public welfare department, Floyd Vann was my step-father.

Our next-door neighbors were white with a bunch of children.

During the week the kids headed to school. The yellow school bus picked up the whites. We walked.

After school and on weekends Black and white kids played baseball, basketball, or football on a vacant lot on their own teams. When either team was short players, we didn't play. Even as kids we were conscious of race and segregation. Blacks and whites could play against one another, but never, never on the same team. Most of the time disputes were settled with a coin toss. But when that didn't work, the difference escalated into name calling:

"Nigger!

"White trash!"

After some pushing and shoving, there was the inevitable fight. One Saturday when Blacks won the fight, a white dad shouted at and cursed the Black kids. Floyd was told and he threatened the white man: "I'm gonna whoop your ass." The white man returned home for his shotgun and Floyd loaded his pistol. The two men were moving into the unpaved streets. It was a showdown reminiscent of a western movie. We looked on approvingly. Both cursed, threatened, and hollered at each other long enough for the police chief, Vernon Glen, to arrive.

Miss Puffins, the old white woman across the street, had called the cops. The "High Noon" shootout was avoided when the police chief demanded that the two men shake hands or go to jail. Both the Black and white kids appeared disappointed that there would be no shootout. After a day or so, the youngsters returned to the playground and proceeded with the segregated games until the next dispute sent them back into racial warfare. Guns and adults never entered the battlefield again.

I remember fondly the first Christmas at our house. Christmas wasn't very special for me. I never believed in Santa Claus; we didn't have a chimney for him to slide down and I didn't think there was a friendly white man. Mama's boss had a son about my age and size. I was given his old clothes, all but the shoes. The shoes went to my brother. Like the white boy, Toote had big feet. Sometimes I got a yo-yo, a spinning top, marbles or those high-class Buster Brown shoes the radio commercials boasted about: "I'm Buster Brown. I live in a shoe. That's my dog, Tige. He lives in there too!" If you didn't own a pair of Buster Brown shoes, you were teased for being really po'.

On the first Christmas in our house, Mama bought a tree and some blinking lights. The kids pasted strips of colored paper into rings and hung them on the tree. When we finished, Floyd stuck an angel on top. He had painted its face black. None of my friends had Black angels on their tree. It seemed odd and so out of place. It was embarrassing.

I loved Sunrise Baptist Church on Christmas Eve. The kids sang, read Bible verses and holiday poems. The Black church is a spiritual rally calling to the flock to hold onto its faith, despite the common suffering. "God is our Redeemer," the preacher reminded us. "He is our refuge and our strength." And for our obedience we would join white angels in Heaven, where pearly gates and streets of gold awaited us.

Sermons in the Black church are a kind of group therapy session highlighting hope. The religious festivities are at their best during Christmas. After Christmas Eve services, Augustine Ryder lined up the kids and we tramped through the neighborhood singing carols. Sometimes we crossed the tracks and sang to white folks. They appeared friendly during the holiday season. That was not so the rest of the year. Adult white folks didn't like colored kids, and sometimes cursed or shouted at us and called us names. I was never afraid of them. After they tried to make us regret just living and breathing, they generally chuckled and moved on.

The holiday merriment year after year has blended into one long happy celebration—with the best of the best of times associated with the never-ending first Christmas in our new home. I wondered then, as I wonder now, why can't every day be like Christmas?

Our lives centered on the church: Sunday services, Wednesday prayer meetings and on Thursday mandatory B.Y.P.U. meetings for the kids. I was an adult before I learned B.Y.P.U. meant Baptist Young People's Union.

Miss Proody always sat in the middle of a back pew at Sunrise Baptist Church, near the glowing, coal-filled potbellied stove. She weighed nearly 300 pounds, gathered from a near-lethal accumulation of pig feet, chitterlings, mashed potatoes, and all things fattening. Her big ears rounded to a point and showed the long gray hair growing inside.

Her ebony face was covered with several layers of makeup and a thin line of lipstick circled the opening where she stuffed the food. A wig in serious need of brushing, straightening, or discarding covered the tiny head set directly on her seemingly neckless shoulders. Miss Proody's body was pushed down by her colossal breasts. She was a nice person, but even so she could have been an oversized double for the Wicked Witch of the West in the *Wizard of Oz*.

It was said if her husband was weighed with his garden plow, he might top a hound's tooth over 100 pounds.

Miss Proody must have had ten cats that roamed outside and as many scattered throughout her shotgun shack. Her junky house, with its dead rat smell, looked like a cotton field, as the fur all those cats shed piled up year after year.

Her church shouting was the closest thing to opera in Vinita. Such clamor is still an art in the Baptist church. The howling requires an age of at least 70 to become proficient. On one unusually boring Sunday morning, I moved into the pew behind her with mischief in mind.

The old woman was predictable. The prayer was offered. She shouted. The choir sang. She shouted. During the beginning and middle of Reverend Dan Harris' threats of fire and brimstone, she shouted.

In what appeared to be his final assault on the Devil, she closed with her most shrilling outburst. Miss Proody's melodious eruption was funnier than Big John and Sparky and Clarabelle the Clown on the Howdy Doody radio shows.

When she stood to shout on this Sunday, I slipped a tack under her seat. Miss Proody sat as the deacons were coming with the collection plate to close the service. Then, 300 pounds of cat fur and ample humanity hurtled upward, rising farther than any Olympic record since Caesar's time. Her moves could only have been choreographed by God. Simultaneously, the old woman let loose the loudest, longest, harmonic squeal in the history of any prayer meeting on all the seven continents. As women rushed to her with fans, Miss Proody's screaming inspired Reverend Harris' attempt to save another soul or two. He must have preached 30 minutes more before the collection plate was finally passed and the fanning brigade returned to their seats. I never sat near her again and her whining tributes to the gospel became less apparent. Too bad.

Now, that was entertainment!

Vinita is still a very special place for me. When I visit the graveyard where Mama and Floyd are buried, I never fail to stop by Miss Proody's plot and many of the others who shaped my early life. My youth was crammed with adventures and learning experiences, but I thank God that those times have also passed on.

2
My Family on the Trail of Tears

Great atrocities are committed against the indigenous people.
                                    Bartolomé de las Casas, 1533

VINITA, INDIAN TERRITORY, was established before the Civil War as a settlement of Freedman and mixed-blood Blacks who marched with the Five Civilized Tribes on the Trail of Tears. Many of the Black settlers were part of a bilingual and a tri-cultural (Black, white and Indian) people, seeking to establish new lives for themselves.

The village was originally named Downingville, after Cherokee Chief Lewis Downing. The chief led a faction opposed to slavery. In this pastoral village, even today, nearly all the old Black families are Cherokee tribal members and descendants of survivors of the Trail of Tears. Blacks of Cherokee ancestry with the Downing surname are still among the Black leaders in Vinita. The Cherokee town was renamed Vinita in honor of Vinnie Ream, a sculptor who created the life-size statue of Lincoln at the United States Capitol. Biographers suggest her "feminine wiles" may have convinced U.S. Senator Edmund Ross of Kansas to deliver the deciding vote against the impeachment of Andrew Johnson. The Vinita name change was spearheaded by Colonel Elias Boudinot II. It was rumored there was a romantic relationship between Boudinot and Ms. Ream.

Colonel Boudinot was the son of a celebrated Cherokee (either a sell-out or patriot, depending on the speaker). His father, born Gulageenah "Buck Deer" Watie, was a brother of Stand Watie. As was Cherokee custom, Gulageenah adopted the name Boudinot from an American Revolutionary patriot and benefactor.

President Andrew Jackson coerced the Watie brothers and 34

others into signing the fraudulent Treaty of New Echota in Georgia in 1835. The pact traded Cherokee ancestral lands for land in what is now Oklahoma, driving the tribe onto the "the trail that cried" in a forced migration in 1838-39.

In his first inaugural address, President Jackson had called upon the tribes to surrender their lands and move to the western territories. Their rights would be considered so far as they were "consistent with the habits of our Government and the feelings of our people." Jackson's position was uncompromising. He wanted the Five Civilized Tribes to be removed or "to disappear and be forgotten."

Threatened with annihilation, the Choctaws and Creek moved to the western territories in the early 1830s. They received hunting and farming equipment and subsistence for one year. After an initial resistance the Chickasaw acquiesced to the banishment and were shoved west.

The Cherokee and Seminole tribes refused to cooperate and waged significant resistance. The Cherokees ultimately were rounded up and unmercifully forced to their new lands under insufferable hardships. Four thousand Cherokees perished from the brutal winter, disease, and hunger.

The Seminoles and their Black tribesmen chose to resist, engaging in a seven-year war. Seminole success in battle was built on alliances with Black tribesmen and slaves who valued their freedom as much as the Seminoles valued their lands. These fierce fighters fled to the Florida swamps, avoided capture, and roamed free for years. A small contingent of the rebellious Black-Indian faction fought well into the 1850s. Their descendants escaped removal to the west and are in Florida today.

Big Mama's great-grandfather, Jacob Bruner, and his kin, William and Affie Bruner, were among the first group who were marched to Indian Territory as slaves. William, John, Caesar, Perry, and Paro Bruner, sons of William and Affie, were later freed and founded the Black village of Brunertown and became Creek and Seminole tribal leaders. Creek and Seminole are the same people. In the Creek language, "Seminole" means "runaway."

Big Mama's grandfather, Joshua Grayson, adopted the surname

of his slave master Watt Grayson. To this day the Grayson and Bruner family names are interchangeable. Some family members kept Bruner, their tribal name, others used Grayson. Big Mama was named for her great-grandmother Mary Ann Grayson, but preferred Bruner, her great-grandfather's tribal name.

For a time, the Bruner family settled on the edge of the Creek Nation that eventually became Seminole land. Caesar Bruner served on the Seminole Tribal Council and was the first leader of a Freedman Band of the tribe that carries his name to this day.

His brother, Paro Bruner, was a prominent Creek leader. He served in the nation's House of Warriors and was a leader of Canadian Colored, one of the earliest Black towns in the territory. He was a scout for federal marshal Bass Reaves, the legendary Black lawman who served under "Hanging" Judge Isaac Parker, whose court ruled over Indian Territory. Reaves would also be involved in the shooting death of Big Mama's grandfather, Joshua Grayson.

According to tribal records, Mitchell and Joshua Grayson were the sons of Mary Ann Grayson and Jacob Bruner. The family's oral tradition says that Mitchell killed Joshua in 1883 in a dispute over a pig. The Creeks shielded Mitchell from arrest by Bass Reaves, since Mitchell had already been tried and acquitted by the tribe. Tribal records report that Mitchell, Joshua, and a sister, Dolly Grayson, were placed on the Creek Nation rolls in 1867; the U.S. courts had no jurisdiction.

Tribal records and oral history concur in that Mitchell married Jeanetta

Grayson, the great-granddaughter of Robert Grierson, a Scottish fur trader who married a Creek Indian of some African blood. Grierson served as interpreter and facilitator between the Creek and white settlers. Over time, the name Grierson became Grayson.

Big Mama's grandparents, Mary Ann and Jacob Grayson, and their children Mitchell and Dolly Grayson were slaves of Grierson's son, Watt Grayson, one of the richest and largest slaveholders in the territory. Even though they were kin, the Creek Graysons owned the land and the Black Graysons plowed the fields.

Big Mama's mother, Liza Bruner, was the daughter of Silla Grayson, a member of the Creek Nation and grandniece of Watt Grayson. My Uncle Ira, Big Mama's son, insisted that the two brothers, Mitchell and Joshua, had therefore married two cousins—Silla and Jeanetta, both relatives of slave master Watt Grayson. These complicated relationships were not unusual among the Five Civilized Tribes.

A court document filed by Big Mama's father, Perry Jones, alleged she "was of Indian blood" even though she is carried on Creek rolls as a Freedman. The slave-holding Grayson's descendants have denied, hidden, and destroyed records of any family bond with Blacks.

While the disenfranchisement of Black Creek tribal members was unfolding, the nation erupted into the Civil War. After the first shot was fired, the tribes were abandoned by the U.S. government and left trapped between Confederate States of Arkansas, Texas, Missouri, and Louisiana. Indian Territory was the crossroads for the rebel supply line.

In May 1861, the Confederate government authorized three Indian regiments. Stand Watie, a Cherokee leader of a pro-slavery faction, sided with the South and was allowed to fight "only in Indian Territory." Each of the Five Civilized Tribes also pledged to fight under the Confederate banner.

Black volunteers, however, were organized first on behalf of the Union. In August 1862, before Lincoln and the nation were ready to accept the notion of Black troops within its ranks, a regiment of Blacks was organized into the 1st Kansas Colored Volunteer Infantry Regiment without federal authorization. (In contrast, the 5th Massachusetts Colored Cavalry, depicted in the movie *Glory*, was not organized until 1864.) Their gallantry was widely reported and ultimately was used to promote Black troops in the Civil War. Many slaves fled the Indian Territory farms and joined the Kansas regiment.

In a signal of things to come, President Abraham Lincoln signed the District of Columbia Compensated Emancipation Act in 1862, ending slavery in the nation's capital. The law freed more than 3,000 slaves and provided compensation to slave owners "loyal to the Union." The U.S. also provided up to $100 for those freed slaves who chose to leave the country.

The Emancipation Proclamation followed, on January 1, 1863.

Word reached Galveston, Texas, on June 19, 1865. The tradition of "the Black 4th of July," or "Juneteenth," was carried by migrating Texas Blacks to Oklahoma and Arkansas, and into nearly 200 communities, many that were untouched by the Civil War. The 1863 proclamation led to Lincoln's reluctant establishment of federally authorized Black regiments.

On July 1, 1863, after Lincoln's proclamation allowing Blacks into the military, a battle occurred at Big Cabin, ten miles from Vinita. The 1st Kansas Colored Infantry crushed Confederate General Watie's warriors. On July 17, 1863, the well-outnumbered colored troops engaged Watie again, in the decisive Battle of Honey Springs near Fort Gibson east of Vinita, completely routing the Indian brigade and making possible the capture of Fort Smith.

The Battle of Honey Springs became known as the "Gettysburg of the West." Union General James G. Blunt said he never saw such fighting as was done by the Negro regiment: "The question that Negroes will fight is settled. Besides, they make better soldiers in every respect than any troops I have ever had under my command." There were 88 Civil War battles fought in Indian Territory.

Historical records report that Big Mama's great-grandfather Jacob Bruner "died during the Civil War." It isn't known if he was a Union soldier or died during the frequent raids of Black villages by Confederate Indian troops.

The Union's deployment of colored infantry ended the South's presence in Indian Territory. The victory cut an important rebel supply line, halting reinforcements from Texas. Among the supplies seized by the Union were hordes of shackles said to be for binding captured Blacks for transport to the South after the assumed victory.

The Confederate War policy on slaves was to take no prisoners. Unarmed Black soldiers were massacred routinely. William Quantrill was discredited even by southern generals for the brutality of his guerillas, including the future bank robber Jesse James, who boasted of murdering 150 Black and Indians. The Five Civilized Tribes didn't end slavery until new treaties were signed two years after General Robert E. Lee surrendered.

When the all-Black 9th and 10th Cavalry Regiments were

organized after the war, many of the former Kansas troops who fought in Indian Territory filled its ranks. They were called "Buffalo Soldiers" by Plains Indians because of their fierce fighting and kinky hair. The Army also officially recognized the "Seminole Negro Indian Scouts." The scouts were awarded three Congressional Medals of Honor. The Buffalo Soldiers built Fort Sill, still operating in Lawton, Oklahoma, and other garrisons throughout the Southwest. Henry O. Flipper, the first Black graduate of West Point, was assigned to the Buffalo Soldiers at Fort Sill. As the post engineer, Flipper constructed a drainage system that eliminated a number of stagnant ponds that had contributed to outbreaks of malaria. "Flipper's Ditch" is now a national historic landmark.

The celebrated Army General John "Black Jack" Pershing received his nickname for commanding these Black troops that hunted Geronimo and chased Pancho Villa. During the Spanish-American War, Buffalo Soldier Sergeant George Berry carried the regiment's colors as they saved Teddy Roosevelt's charge up San Juan Hill in Cuba. The Buffalo Soldiers earned 23 Medals of Honor.

Black troops are credited with opening the West for white settlers who were often hostile to them. The unassigned lands of Indian Territory were opened in historic land runs beginning in 1889. Blacks were among the thousands who took part in the dramatic race to stake out a homestead and nearly 40 all-Black towns were organized. Black leaders began promoting that Oklahoma enter the union as a Black state.

As the movement for statehood gained impetus, Democrats fanned white fears with the threat of Oklahoma as a Black state. Democrats promised that, if given control of the 1906 constitutional convention where the state's constitution would be drafted, they would put Blacks in their place.

Ultimately, Republicans adopted the Democrats' race baiting tactics and abandoned Blacks. The party of Lincoln was abandoning its legacy. In the end, the GOP lost the Blacks and didn't gain white bigots. When the votes were counted, the Democrats controlled the constitutional convention. Republicans would remain in Oklahoma's political wilderness until 2005 when the GOP assumed the majority in the Oklahoma House of Representatives and held a 48-48 tied membership in the state Senate. The next election brought control of both legislative houses to the Republicans and, in 2010, the governor's seat as well.

In achieving statehood, Oklahoma had not only joined the Union, but also unified into the collective of southern racism. The first bill passed by the Oklahoma Legislature was the infamous Senate Bill One, which rigidly segregated the state. Miscegenation laws were codified and Indian were declared as white, further complicating Black-Indian relations. Marriage between Blacks and Indians was now illegal. A clash between these "uppity" Oklahoma Blacks and callous whites was encoded in the new state's political landscape.

As a consequence of fighting on behalf of the Confederacy, new treaties with the tribes were written. Blacks were declared citizens of the Indian nations and as such received land allotments. The Dawes Commission, designed to establish tribal memberships, enrolled many Blacks with Indian blood as "Freedmen." Big Mama's mother, the dark-skinned Liza Bruner, was categorized as a "mulatto" on one census and a Freedman on the Dawes Rolls. Today, tribes are challenging the tribal membership of Freedmen.

In time, Oklahoma became a virtual proving ground for civil rights decisions before the U.S. Supreme Court, as the "Old South" intransigence crept into the state. At the turn of the century, the resurgence of the Klan and its unregulated violence, lynching, court-licensed discrimination, and burning of Black communities made the Tulsa Race Riot inevitable.

3
Oklahoma: A Black Blessing?

The nature of the American Society is such that we are prevented from knowing who we are.
                                                                Ralph Ellison

AFTER THE CIVIL WAR, Indian Territory was seen as The Promised Land for many Blacks searching for economic survival and for those fleeing southern oppression. Freedmen came from the North and former slaves from the Deep South. College-trained professionals from northern universities, farmers, and many others came with skills learned in bondage to gather in the Promised Land. They mixed with Blacks who had been marched to the land on the Trail of Tears.

They came to the territory with hopeful expectation and diverse traditions, but sharing in common a desperate desire to escape the intense persecution.

The restrictive racial lines in the territory were to a degree ambiguous. More all-Black towns were established in The Promised Land than in any state in the union. Some began as villages adjacent to Indian settlements. Others were developed by pioneering Blacks after the land rush. Black villages and towns in Oklahoma include: Alsuma, Arcadia, Arkansas Colored (may have also been known as Tuskegee), Bailey, Boley, Bookertee, Chase, Canadian Colored, Clearview, Downingville (later Vinita), Ferguson, Foreman, Gibson Station, Grayson (formerly Wildcat), Lewisville, Lima, Lincoln City Liberty, Marshalltown, Overton, Red Bird, Rentieville, Rentie Grove, Summit, Taft, Tatum, Tullahassee, Vernon, Wellston Colony, Wewoka, Wiley, Wybark, and Langston.

My maternal great-grandmother and my grandmother were born

in the Black settlement of North Fork Colored. They also lived in Canadian Colored and Wewoka, a village established by Black Creek.

North Fork Colored neighbored the Creek Indian Settlement of North Fork, near present day Eufaula in McIntosh County. The area was a strategic supply base for the Confederates during the Civil War. The Corps of Engineers flooded the town to create Lake Eufaula in 1946.

The Bruner clan—including William and Affie Bruner's sons William, John, Caesar, Perry, Davis, and Paro—established "Brunertown" in Hughes County, a place all but lost in Oklahoma history. My family also established the Freedman villages of Huttonville, Turkey Creek, and Prairies Edge. Paro Bruner represented the Black town of Canadian Colored in the Creek House of Warriors.

In the South, whites' antipathy toward former slaves was enforced with hostility and by violence. Inside the Promised Land, 71 percent of Black farmers owned their land and exercised political clout as Republicans. They had divisions among themselves. Southern Black settlers were perceived as more yielding to white hostility and were frowned upon by Freedmen. Territorial Blacks were of a more independent spirit and less inclined to accept the social expectations of the sons of the Confederacy. The former slaves' modest achievement—rising from slavery to sharecropping—still left them in a position similar to their status before the war.

Nevertheless, these Black settlements included all philosophical stripes, and offered education, self-determination, and freedom from whites' racial rules. Blacks were not pushed into the isolation; they deliberately and voluntarily sought and embraced the ethnic quarantine of Black towns. These shelters, this cathartic act of self-segregation, served not only to reveal and affirm Blacks as worthy citizens to whites, but established as much to themselves.

E.P. McCabe was the leading advocate of all-Black towns. He migrated from Kansas, where he had been elected as state auditor. After the Oklahoma Land Rush, McCabe acquired 320 acres near Guthrie and established Langston in 1892. McCabe was active in Republican politics and was named an assistant auditor in the territorial government. He encouraged Black migration as "free farmers" who would outnumber whites.

McCabe pressed President Benjamin Harrison to bring Indian Territory into the union as an all-Black state with himself installed as its governor. The *Republic*, a Washington D.C. newspaper, reported in 1890 that the sudden departure of McCabe from Kansas meant he had assurances from President Harrison that he would be made governor. "Machinery is now in motion that will land 40,000 or 50,000 Negroes voters," the paper said. The *Kansas City Times* estimated the racial breakdown of the territory that year as 25,000 whites and 15,000 Blacks.

According to a *New York Times* article published on February 28, 1890, an official said there was much bitterness over McCabe's candidacy for governor and, if it became fact, McCabe would "be assassinated within a week after he enters the Territory." The newspaper noted that there was a rapidly growing anti-Negro sentiment, prompted by the aggressiveness of Blacks, and it would unite the whites, "and Oklahoma will possibly be seeing the beginning of a race war."

A leading Republican reported a white man as saying he was told a dead nigger makes an excellent fertilizer. "If Negroes try to Africanize Oklahoma, they will find that we will enrich our soil with them."

Even so, Frederick Douglass, the aging abolitionist, said that Oklahoma Territory could be a Black man's blessing.

The arrogance of racism would shape the debate on Oklahoma's statehood, influence the period following the Constitutional Convention, and set in motion racial segregation as the rule of law in the new state.

After statehood, McCabe left Oklahoma and settled in Chicago. He died a pauper in 1929. His widow buried him in Topeka, Kansas, attending the graveside ceremony with only the undertaker and gravedigger.

McCabe's legacy remains today. From 1865 to 1920 African-Americans created more than 50 identifiable towns and settlements, with 13 still in existence in Oklahoma. Oklahoma's unique history of first being an Indian Territory and coming late to statehood gave rise to the hopes of self-determination for African-American who had arrived first with the Trail of Tears and then as freedmen and women following the Civil War. Strict Jim Crow segregation in Tulsa led to the formation of the Greenwood community on Tulsa's North Side. Accessibility of open land, a lot which was close to the largest city of Eastern Oklahoma, gave rise to this urban community and to multiple all-Black townships, some of which still exist today.

The towns of Clearview, Vernon, Langston, Brooksville, Grayson, Lima, Boley, Tatums, Rentiesville, Red Bird, Taft, Summit, and Tullahassee still have noted populations on the 2010 census.

Five years after Edwin McCabe founded Langston in 1982, he influenced the establishment of the Colored Agricultural and Normal University, later named Langston University. Today Langston University has an enrollment of over 3000 students, with campuses in both Greenwood and Oklahoma City.

Boley is the largest of the all-Black towns of Oklahoma. Like most rural towns in Oklahoma, they suffered through hard times in the 1930s, causing a decline in population. Today Boley is still famous for the African-American community-based rodeo it features every Memorial Day.

Rentiesville, located 17 miles southwest of Muskogee, is famous for its music tradition. It was the home of the late famed bluesman D.C. Minner and his Dust 'Til Dawn Blues Festival, which is held each year in Rentiesville.

The combined existence of these Black townships, alongside the urban existence of Greenwood, led to historic African-American economic development and self-determination in Oklahoma.

4
Bloodline: Thicker Than Water

But what of Black women? I doubt if any other race of women could have brought its fineness up through so devilish a fire.
                                                                                W.E.B. DuBois

BIG MAMA NEVER LET US FORGET our Creek heritage, but I found out about my Cherokee blood during a casual conversation with a friend on a trip to Langston. Mama had told us we were kin to the House family. I paid little attention. I have a great many friends whom I now call "cous," because old folks confirmed some kinship. In most cases we don't have the foggiest notion of how our bloodlines are connected. Over the years, Big Mama and Aunt Mildred had linked us to many families—but in the case of the Houses, it turned out to be true.

A friend, Millard House, was a Tulsa school administrator. We were attending a meeting at Langston University and were to have dinner with his sister, Viola, who was the mayor of the town. En route I told House Mama's story of our family relationship. "Viola is the family historian and she will know," he answered. On arriving, House repeated my story to his sister. "Get in the car," she shouted excitedly. We drove to nearby Guthrie. Pearliner House, a 103-year old, slender-built woman opened the door. When I told her who I was, she embraced me.

"Lawdy mercy, you're Mary Ann's grandbaby." Her smiling face had sharply chiseled features, high cheekbones, thin lips, a narrow nose and the steady balance of a woman much younger. Her hair was gray, braided and long. For any discerning eyes, the fair-skinned Pearliner House was an Indian.

My great-grandmother, Liza Bruner, married Aunt Pearliner's

brother, Perry Jones. Perry's dad, Mose Jones, settled on land still owned by family members in Langston and married a Cherokee woman named Pearl. Langston was much ballyhooed as a Black Mecca of freedom at that time, thanks to the advocacy of E.P. McCabe. My great-great-grandfather apparently heard of the success stories of Oklahoma Blacks.

Photographs of Grandma Liza, Grandpa Perry, Mose Jones, Big Mama and two great-great aunts covered the wall above her sofa. My mama had been named "Pearline" after her. Aunt Pearliner and Big Mama had remained in contact by writing letters.

"My dad came to Oklahoma after the Civil War," Aunt Pearliner noted. "I hate the Cherokees. They cheated us out of our land and our heritage." Her mother Pearl was a full-blood Cherokee. "I am Black," she protested.

When I asked my grandmother why she never told us about Aunt Pearliner, she simply replied: "You never asked."

There is an interesting contrast between my grandmother and Aunt Pearliner. My grandmother lived among whites in Vinita and prided herself as an Indian. Aunt Pearliner lived in a Black town and had nothing but disdain for Indians.

The Dawes Commission's official U.S. policy divided the tribes into full-bloods, mixed-bloods and Freedmen. While examining my grandmother's papers after her death, I found her Creek Enrollment Card listing her as a "Freedman." The same was so for Grandma Liza.

Big Mama was 93 when she died in 1993. I wrote in her obituary: "Mary Ann Jones' roots were well planted in pre-statehood Oklahoma's soil. She is an eternal link that connects one generation's Indian heritage with the other. It is through her that this family is bound with that history."

Attending her funeral was Leona Bruner Masters, the daughter of Rayford Bruner, Grandma Liza's half-brother through her father, Joshua Grayson. Leona invited me to her home and shared much of the family's Indian history. She explained that the Graysons and Bruners were the same family. Indeed, Grandma Liza's 1896 Creek census card lists Joshua Grayson as her father, but notes she is on the 1890 census as "Liza Bruner," the revered family name Grandma Liza and my grandmother preferred.

As white mixed-bloods became tribal leaders and chiefs, they disfranchised mixed-blood Blacks, many of whom were their kin. Before and after the Civil War, Blacks were exiled socially and by tribal law. Historical accounts tell the story of Robert Grierson (also known as Grayson), the patriarch of the Grayson family, disinheriting his daughter, Katie, who had children by a Black man, until she rid herself of him. She remarried a white man and began vanquishing their African heritage, as did all the other Graysons. The Graysons established a racist legacy in Oklahoma. Washington Grayson served as a captain in the Confederate Army. Ironically, the all-Black town of Grayson, Oklahoma, is still named for this slave-owner.

The cultural banishment was also underway with the Five Civilized Tribes. Historical accounts and my family's experience confirmed for me the Five Civilized Tribes were artificially white and effectively racist. The Oklahoma tribes were the only Indians who held Black slaves. Blacks who proudly boast of "Indian blood" are associating themselves with the slaveholding Five Civilized Tribes. It is an ironic historical twist that the Buffalo Soldiers "cleared the west" of Plains Indians, who, unlike their civilized cousins in Oklahoma, never held Blacks as slaves.

It's repugnant to me that the Five Civilized Tribes assumed the racist practices of the very people who had stolen their land, contaminated their culture, offended their humanity, and placed the tribes on the torturous Trail of Tears.

Not every branch of these tribes was discriminatory. Factions of the Seminole Nation were more tolerant of Black tribal members. Near the end of the 20th century, Blacks served on the Seminole tribal council.

Leona linked us to other Black families and to "Aunt" Dolly Grayson Stidham, the sister of Joshua Grayson who had raised my grandmother for a time. Leona said the Creek Bruners and Seminole Bruners are the same families, scattered throughout Northeastern Oklahoma. Slaves, Indians, and Black tribal members often entered into what she called "sanctioned marriages" with little ceremony and when broken up, the spouses went their separate ways, often to enter into another sanctioned marriage. "They just started new families who recognized each other as kin," Leona explained.

Without a hint of this relationship, I had included Dolly Stidham's striking photograph in a historical exhibit for The Greenwood Cultural Center. Her photograph was featured in a Works Progress Administration project after the Great Depression. The family relationship was also confirmed later by my Uncle Ira Jones, who saw the photograph while visiting the center.

When Leona died, as I entered the church I noticed my barber, Willie Sells, who had just cut my hair that morning. Unknown to us, we were both kin to Leona. Rayford Bruner's mother Sonja Jones was Sell's father's sister. Another group of longtime friends was added to my "cous" list.

Mama had always told us Big Mama once "had a bunch of land in Okmulgee." I found the record of her 160-acre Creek allotment and travelled to the Okmulgee County Courthouse to examine the records. Despite tribal resistance against land allotments for Freedmen, Grandma Liza, and her infant children (Big Mama and her brothers, Willie and George) received land allotments. Their father, Perry Jones, was assigned as their guardian.

Until I gained a court order, Big Mama's probate records had been closed and never reviewed for nearly a century. The record told the story of how her land was legally stolen.

The Congressional Act of 1908 transferred probate issues of the Five Civilized Tribes from the U.S. Department of the Interior to Oklahoma's state courts. Each county established its own rules on guardianship for minor tribal children. It was federal law that state courts could assign a guardian to handle the affair of Freedmen who had not reached the age of majority.

With the discovery of oil in the county, Big Mamma's land attracted white managers who could sell or lease the land and its mineral rights under very lenient courts. Before the court records showed otherwise, I was convinced that Big Mama's father, Perry, had masterminded some kind of shady deal to sell her land. After all, he was the guardian of record and by all accounts Jones was a bit of a rascal. As it turned out, I was wrong. Big Mama had fallen prey to a government-sanctioned hustle to legally steal millions of dollars in land and mineral rights from Freedmen and mixed-blood Blacks under the age of majority.

Freedmen under the age of majority were hauled into court to show cause why "a competent guardian" should not be appointed to handle their affairs. "Professional guardians" were unique to the Oklahoma Indian land allotment process that resulted from the Civil War. They were most always white chiselers in complete control of any proceedings regarding the sale or lease of the land. Excessive commissions, attorney and other fees and downright theft of the land were common practices.

In many cases, the guardians were less educated and less competent than were the parents of these "wards of the court." An "incompetence" rationale for the thievery was written into the 1908 congressional act and was used as a vehicle by the local courts and their allies to steal or assume control of land held by minor children of Freedmen. The court named J.E. Porter, an Okmulgee physician and oil and gas speculator, as Big Mama's guardian. Porter first sold her mineral rights and then her land.

Porter was entitled by law to ten percent of any financial transaction and the same for the lease or sale of the land. Monthly accounting of expenses owed to the guardian were often more than the land's revenue. According to probate records, Porter sold Big Mama's land in 1911 for $1,855. More than $1,200 was charged off as expenses of the professional guardian, leaving her with less than $700. Grandma Liza and Grandpa Perry had no say in the theft of their daughter's property.

Grandpa Jones had protested the land sale in a petition filed from prison. Jones was called Pennyman, so nicknamed because he shot a man in a dice game dispute over a penny bet. In 1910, he began a five-year sentence for assault and attempted murder. He served three years in state prison and was paroled in 1913.

In opposing the sale, he declared his daughter also had an inherited 40 acres of land from her dead brother. He said it was good farmland "and in good state of cultivation and if properly handled will bring an income from $75 to $100 a year."

Grandpa Jones wrote in his petition to the court that his daughter "is of Indian blood" and the land was part of U.S. treaties and her heritage. He insisted that the current oil leases on the 160 acres was sufficient for needs. This is also the only record, other than the family's oral history, that confirmed my grandmother was indeed of "Indian blood" and should have been placed on the Creek rolls. As such, Jones argued that the only expense the guardian was legally bound to pay was $6.00 per month for board and schooling. Big Mama resided with her great aunt Dolly Grayson Stidham and, according to her father, she did not require any expenses other than her clothing.

"The father and next of kin demands that the said land 'not be sold,'" he petitioned the judge. He also asked the court to require the guardian to report the money and show an accounting of the expenses. Jones' petition was thrown out of court. E. H. Moore was one of the men who bought Big Mama's land, rich in oil and gas. Moore, partnering with W.B. Pine, formed an oil company and gathered other oil leases. Their company was eventually valued at $25 to $40 million. The company was sold to Phillips Petroleum Company in 1929. Both men became U.S. Senators representing Oklahoma. Pine's campaign was actively supported by the Ku Klux Klan.

Over the years, the land was swapped from one major oil company to another. The rusting natural gas pumps and oil derricks still stand as monuments to the depleted wealth siphoned from the land allotment and to our family's generations of poverty, victims of illiteracy and the law.

The outrageous professional guardianship practice in Oklahoma inspired Blacks to form the Negro Guardianship League. Although they won some challenges, the organization had little success in halting the wholesale practice of court-approved burglary. Even though Blacks valued land over all other possessions, professional guardianships diminished the already limited opportunities for Freedmen.

My aunt's anger can be justified in that our family never benefited from the profits taken from the stolen land and stolen legacy.

While her guardian had sold her land allotment, Big Mama still had her 80 acres of land inherited from her brother Willie. Big Mama and her brother George each held an undivided interest in the 160-acre allotment left to her by Willie. In 1919, Big Mama was nineteen, in control of her property, and out of the clutches of thieves—maybe. The signatures of Mary Ann Jones and her husband, Isaac Evitt, are on a bill of sale for her 80 acres, shortly after the Tulsa riot. It was sold to A.D. Kennedy, one of Okmulgee's most prominent citizens. This is likely the transaction for which my aunt insists that my grandfather, with another woman, forged Big Mama's signature. However, Big Mama may have been left with the oil and mineral rights. If that is so, she never told anybody.

In the mid-1980s, after I was elected to the Oklahoma legislature, Big Mama came to Tulsa from her home in Okmulgee for a month-long stay with Mama. I offered to have the legislative staff examine her oil leases to determine if she was being paid fairly. She left the next day without notice and never visited Tulsa again.

Mama ordered any talk of Big Mama's land to stop. "She's been cheated all her life —her husband, her daddy, big shots, white folks, and she don't trust anybody. Can you blame her?" Mama asked. I couldn't and I never mentioned her land to her again.

5
Black Wall Street's Dark Side

Take me back to Tulsa. Take me to Archer and Greenwood to hear the music and dance the nights away.

                                        Bob Wills, country singer

MAMA, FLOYD VANN, my two brothers, a new baby sister, and I moved from Vinita back to Tulsa in 1952. Mama and Floyd had found good jobs. He fixed flats and pumped gas. She illegally moonlighted as a domestic. Because Mama received welfare, she violated at least four government rules: She worked on the side. There was a man living in our house. She owned a car and had a telephone.

Floyd was proud of the three boys he had rescued from homelessness and raised as his own. He held a fifth-grade education. He told us that when his mother packed him off to school through the front door, before she left the grounds, he escaped through the back entrance to a nearby pond to fish the day away. Nevertheless, he insisted that my brothers and I absorb the tiny bit that was forced on him. When I eclipsed his learning, he proudly announced, "From now on, I will learn from you." It never happened. I was always his student.

While a telephone was not allowed by the welfare department, Mama worked for several families and needed the money. The four-person "party line" would ring on or off the hook. When the welfare caseworker knocked on the door my job was to grab the phone, run to a closet and cover it with a pillow to muffle any ring.

We moved into a crowded apartment complex with hordes of kids. The initiation for a new dude in the projects was to fight. He didn't have to win, but he had to fight. I had drawn Hobart, "the sissy," and was pleased. As a tough bully from Vinita, this would be an easy path to glory and status. We had to remain in a circle drawn around us in the dirt. A chip was placed on Hobart's shoulder and I was dared to knock it off. I did and the fight began. The first one to scream "uncle" lost.

My left uppercut missed. Then Hobart charged me with cycles of windmill swings that connected on both my eyes, my nose, and my top lips—and covered in blood the other parts of my face that he had missed. I was too proud to say uncle. I just raised my hands in surrender and crawled out of the circle. Hobart became my friend and from that day I overlooked any bias against what we called sissies.

My brother Toote had a temper. Oyama, allegedly the toughest cat in his class, was to welcome my brother to the neighborhood. He pushed my brother. In violation of the rules, and to my surprise, Toote walked off as the crowd laughed. Minutes later, he returned to the battle with a large limb better described as a small tree.

As he whapped Oyama, the bully must have hollered uncle for five minutes before Toote's arm tired. Nobody had told my brother "uncle" meant "I surrender." From that fateful day until now, nobody messes with Toote. I can't remember my brother ever having another fight. His reputation was sealed that day when he was 10 years old. Today he's a mild-mannered deacon in his church and an avid hunter. He owns at least 15 weapons and cuts his yard, behind an eight-foot fence, with a 38 pistol in his pocket. Our baby brother says that if anybody jumped that fence, he would hurry them on that journey of endless nights and then pray for their soul.

The projects were twelve four-family apartments that housed about 500 men, women, and children. What we called the old neighborhood was several blocks of poverty centered by the pride of the Black community, Booker T. Washington High School. In the cool of the evening, old folks sat outside, watched the kids at play and vanquished troublemaking strangers by threatening to "call the police."

The lone whites in the neighborhood operated what Blacks called the "Jew Store." The Napfeh family that operated it were actually Lebanese. They extended credit for overpriced groceries until the first of the month, when "the check" came from the government. On weekends, another familiar white plagued the projects. In his shiny new

Buick, the bootlegger only dealt with cash customers. Oklahoma, along with Mississippi, was a totally "dry" state.

I don't know if Mama ever had a key to the front door, or remember anybody's place being robbed. I am convinced neighborhood crime came with air conditioning; the old folks left their front porch look-out and glued themselves to the TV watching "Search for Tomorrow," "Gunsmoke," and "Wagon Train" instead.

Poverty does breed industry. We traded spare parts to keep our bicycles repaired and built homemade scooters from old skates and wood stolen in the evening from Henshaw's Lumber Company bordering the 'hood. Apparently, Mr. Henshaw began missing the boards and placed a vicious and loud German police dog in the yard at night.

The dog was a problem for a while, but then we figured out a plan. We threw the animal Spam and potted meat, free food given to poor folks by the county. After three or four days, the dog welcomed our visits. He became so friendly that T.J. Wilson pulled the fence up and took him home.

Years later, I served in the Oklahoma Legislature with Jim Henshaw, the lumber yard owner's son. I told him the story. He said when his dad realized we were kids and not stealing much, that Mr. Henshaw removed the dog. I never told Jim that T.J. called the hound "Scooter."

In the 'hood, discipline was serious. Any parent in the projects was authorized to render a spanking to anybody's child caught in mischief on the spot. I once stole an apple from Peevy's Grocery Store. En route home I felt guilty and decided to return it. The apple was stuck in my pocket. Peevy saw me, pulled off his belt, whipped me out of his store and called my mama. She met me on the trail and whipped me home with a clothes iron cord. I have never stolen since.

We were more than poor. We were po'. Reaching the so-called poverty line was something for our families to aspire to. When the federal government's urban renewal came to Tulsa, the first area bulldozed was my old neighborhood. Yet the projects had character and all the fabric of achievement.

Only a very few kids dropped out of high school. Many went

to college and became teachers, a lawyer, a doctor, college professors, a college president, policemen, entrepreneurs, social workers, mechanics, a journalist, and two state senators and three state representatives. Mama was part of the compact for success. A high school drop-out, she saw school as a way to get to the other side of tracks.

Mama was a younger, less portly look-alike of Big Mama and a generous, enterprising lady. Every room in our place was always packed with relatives, friends and sometimes total strangers down on their luck.

They slept in the kitchen, on the floor, and even on pillows and blankets piled in the bathtub. The people sleeping in the bathtub were awakened often and pushed outside when the many had to use it. She had a hand in raising and caring for my cousin Mary and Mary's children, and adopted Ben Rickitt, who was mentally challenged and two other orphaned teenagers.

She did much with little. Mama preached that "being po'" was a question of acceptance and was not defined by the lack of wealth. "You ain't poor until you give up," she would say, "and I ain't given up yet." Her reward for things well done was having done them. "You can make it if you try" was more than lyrics of an old blues song; it was her strength, her character, and her legacy to her children.

Mama was also a five-star welfare cheater and an expert at survival and gathering government handouts. To hijack the free groceries given to poor folks by the county, she used various aliases: Pearline Evitt, Ross, or Vann, adding Opal sometimes to expand the list of name combinations and collect more of the free food called "commodities." Our cupboard was filled with the free cheese, sugar, powdered milk, real butter, canned fruit cake, potted meat, Spam and surplus military rations. When money ran short, the extra commodities were sold.

In addition to washing, ironing, and cooking for white folks, at night Mama operated a juke joint where laborers dropped much of their hard-earned cash before they staggered home. She loved to dance and had as much enjoyment as her customers—the fun I suspect she lost in her youth as a teenager raising her kids. A mother at 15, Mama was required to become an adult before her time, thanks to my arrival in 1941.

She was also the enforcer for Floyd's loan sharking business. He loaned money to drunks for a dollar interest on five dollars borrowed. They then bought more of Mama's overpriced half-pints of cheap bourbon. If borrowers couldn't pay off the full loan, they were obligated to pay Floyd the weekly interest. Mama packed a gun. When the debt was not paid, she went looking for the chiseler. "I won't kill you, but I'll shoot off your big toe," she warned. Apparently, offenders did not want to limp around town on nine toes. There were few defaults on the notes.

Mama and Floyd were married when my baby brother "Huck" was no longer eligible for welfare, although it wasn't as premeditated as that.

While I was home on leave from the Air Force, the family was celebrating her birthday. I asked Floyd when he and Mama were getting married. I don't think it had seriously occurred to them.

He responded, "Why buy the cow when you can get the milk free."

Mama exploded. Apparently, the milk suddenly dried up. Before I reported to duty, Mama gained a new alias: Mrs. Pearline "Opal" Vann.

Shortly after we moved to Tulsa, Floyd offered the kids our first glimpse of the bright lights on and around Greenwood. Unlike Vinita, where we had white neighbors, Tulsa was rigidly segregated.

Our tour passed Tipton's Barbecue. Tipton's was Black-owned and segregated. Whites were welcome, but Blacks had to order their ribs from a side window. They were not allowed inside the premises. Floyd's Packard slowly cruised by the YMCA. Scattered along the route were many small businesses, shops, and stores, and two large schools, each covering a four-square block area. We were mesmerized as Floyd announced, "We ain't got to Greenwood yet."

Music and down-home blues pounded against every tight corner and the smell of what could only be called "soul food"—chicken, chitterlings, pig feet, pork chops, and other delicacies— from several restaurants blended into the evening air. Flashing neon lights with a rainbow of vivid colors invited customers into the houses of ghetto cuisine. We were now on Greenwood Avenue.

The street was anchored by Latimer's Barbeque on the north and The Small Hotel on the south, both considered the largest such Black business establishments in the nation. On the mile-long Black boulevard called Greenwood Avenue, the Greenwood Chamber of Commerce business directory of the day listed 42 hotels and rooming houses, 64 restaurants, 52 beauty and barbershops, two cab companies, three movie theaters, 21 professional buildings housing doctors, lawyers, dentists, and other professions, four hospitals and health clinics, two cosmetology schools, two newspapers, a savings and loan, several shoe shine parlors, bars, night clubs, construction contractors, two clerical schools, 75 grocery stores, two jewelry stores, seven pool halls, five photographic studios, a skating rink, and 11 drug stores. Scattered among them were chili parlors, tailors, fruit and hamburger stands, and all kinds of enterprise catering to the needs of an all-Black consumer base. In an earlier time, there was a Black-owned airline piloting two twin-engine planes.

The two-, three-, five- and ten-story red brick buildings were crammed in, the rows broken only by fine homes, the many churches, and wooden shacks in various states of disrepair. Despite the enforced partition, the symbolism allowed Floyd to bathe himself in pride: "All this is owned by coloreds."

Thursday, "maid's day off," became the universal holiday for thousands of maids, butlers, chauffeurs, cooks, and others domestics. They congregated on the Black Wall Street for fun and leisure and to transfer their hard-earned dollars for the services and merchandise that were offered.

Women pranced down the boulevard in their fineries, closely eyed by the men about town who were wearing suits of all colors and shades, with gold watch chains draped from their vest pockets.

It may have been the Black Wall Street by day, but at night Greenwood was a red-light district with gambling halls, juke joints, and carousing ladies of the evening and well-dressed salesmen peddling illegal contraband.

The discrimination stimulated pride and unity. Black dollars were trapped on Greenwood and turned over many, many times. For Black Wall Street entrepreneurs and professionals, the racial isolation was profitable.

Floyd retired to dutifully care for Mama for more than ten years after she was crippled by a debilitating stroke. He died in 1995, five years after Mama passed. He and Mama are buried in Vinita surrounded by family members and their friends, who had packed my early childhood with enchanting adventures in my audition for adulthood.

As a teenager, I also learned the economic segregation was not enough to rid the white community of their addiction to racism. The towering accomplishment of which Floyd was so proud had once been reduced to rubble. When I learned of the Tulsa race riot, I discovered that Floyd was not only celebrating a triumph on Greenwood, but the resilience of a people. The enormity of the resilience can be measured by the completeness of the destruction and the failed pillage of their hope.

6
Tale of a Race War

Blacks who settled in Tulsa had been run out of everywhere. They would run no more! This was their promised land. This was their home and their new life.   Dr. John Hope Franklin

WHILE ATTENDING CRISPUS ATTUCKS Elementary School in Vinita, Mrs. Clara Hardwick, my 5th and 6th grade teacher, said I had shown some ability in writing. But when "the brothers" teased me about trying to be smart—"You think you's white?"—I abandoned my early prose. I began my cover-up with loud silliness and playing "the dozens," the uncouth art of speaking immorally of another's mother: "Yo' mama is so skinny she can walk thro' rain without getting wet." I became known for little else. I was hopelessly ordinary and proudly inadequate.

By high school, I was a loud, attention-seeking, obnoxious clown. I had a well-rehearsed swagger, each step choreographed with a high hand swinging and a cute bounce with each step. I practiced this not-too-novel stride to draw girls. I was a D- student in the required academic subjects, even in gym where all you had to do is show up. I was flunking vocational training, study hall, and romance.

I was awkward when I attempted to jiggle around the dance floor. I even hummed off key. My gravelly voice disrupted the choir so much so that the music teacher offered a passing grade if I exchanged her class for the library. I couldn't dance, sing, or dribble a basketball. Black stereotypes just didn't fit.

A FRONT TOOTH WAS MISSING, thanks to playmate Peewee's lucky punch in one of the many Vinita fights when I had almost always beat up on him. The gap was partially hidden behind the big lips of a mouth almost always filled with Juicy Fruit Chewing Gum. My squinty eyes and oversized ears pointed away from a head thickly covered with kinky hair that refused to be waved unless packed with Vaseline and worked with a hot straightening comb. Other than that, I was perfect.

William David Williams, respectfully called "Mr. W.D." by students, was looking for writers to prepare Booker T. Washington's High School's annual yearbook. The tall, thin beauty for whom I often practiced my signature strut suggested that I volunteer. Many of my hokey poems had been inspired by this passion for her.

I showed up for the class, eager to further impress my gorgeous dream girl. Mr. W.D.'s long-winded yearbook orientation didn't exactly stir me—not at first. "The Booker T. (Washington High School) yearbook is more than a year-to-year diary of school activities," he explained. "It is a chronicle of the history of community as well."

He was short, mild-mannered, and distinguished looking—what old folks called "well-bred." Behind his back, students called him "Headmo." With a few strands of hair stretched across his receded hairline, a large football-shaped head more than over-balanced his small, erect frame. The teacher's horn-rimmed glasses only camouflaged the small eyes anchored on each side of his broad nose, highlighted by a neatly trimmed mustache.

I slumped into my chair, disinterested, as the teacher talked of local history. O.W. Gurley was the founder of the Negro Wall Street of America and one of the richest men in the Territory that was to become Oklahoma.

"Back then many Negroes had money," Mr. W.D. explained. "By 1918, Blacks in Oklahoma (and especially in Tulsa) led the U.S. in ownership of real estate, personal property, and educational progress. Booker T. Washington School, with grades one through twelve, opened in 1913 with six teachers. The school provided the manpower that replenished the pioneering businesses in Tulsa's Black satellite.

Back then? I was not impressed. In modern time, Dr. William N. Coots built an entire neighborhood just below the high school and the Mann Brothers did the same farther south across Lansing and against the railroad tracks. Simon Berry operated a cab company, a bus line, a movie theater, and a skating rink, and owned and flew an airplane. Berry also developed one of two parks in town open to Blacks.

Alphonzo Williams, said to be the richest Black man in town, operated a numbers racket, a cab stand, and a grocery store. He owned a big house and the Rose Room, a popular nightclub where he hired big name entertainment like Count Basie, Duke Ellington, Ike and Tina Turner, Della Reese, Billy Eckstine, Cab Calloway and other stars. The performers generally stayed at Wellington Small's 65-room, three-story hotel.

One day I hoped to own a pool hall and operate a policy wheel, the ghetto racket similar to today's lottery. Select three winning numbers from 15 or so drawn randomly and a dime wagered could bring $10 from the numbers runners who collected the bets. Policy is a ghetto sport, a lottery without government interference. When my grandmother was teased about her gambling "on the wheel" as it was called, she responded, "When I win, I give 10 percent to the Lord."

Negro Wall Street? No big deal. This was boring. I slowly pulled my skinny legs under me to stand and leave at the first rhetorical intermission. But then his slow, laboring voice stopped me cold in my tracks. Mr. W.D. said on the evening of May 31, 1921, the school's graduation ceremonies and prom were cancelled after Dick Rowland, a dropout who worked downtown shining shoes was jailed, accused of raping a white woman—"on a public elevator in broad daylight."

An angry white mob soon gathered at the courthouse intent on lynching the shoe shine boy. Black World War I veterans took up arms and paraded to the courthouse to confront the mob and to protect Rowland. A scuffle between a Black and a white man ensued. A shot rang out. The crowd scattered. A race riot had broken out. Mr. W.D. claimed Blacks defended their community for a while, "but then the airplanes came, dropping bombs." The entire Black community was burned to the ground. As many as 300 people were killed.

Now more annoyed than bored, I leaped from my chair. Enough was enough! "Greenwood was never burned," I shouted. "Ain't never been no 300 people killed. We're too old for fairytales." A 15-year-old calling a teacher a liar was a capital offense. The room's bone-chilling silence was enough to suggest that I lost what little sense I had.

"Sit down, fat mouth," Mr. W.D. snorted, his own mouth twisted with anger. He returned to his hyperbole.

After the class was dismissed, word spread quickly. Classmates avoided me. I was in "trou—bull!" Trouble at school meant trouble at home. Talking back to an adult was a crime where double jeopardy was not only legal, but expected. The likely sentence: a spanking at school and a beating at home. Yearbook activity was extracurricular. I could just quit and remain the school jester, or I could return, face Mr. W.D., apologize, and accept the consequences. But why should I be punished for his brainwashing?

"No buddy. Not me!"

Still undecided the next day, I flipped a coin: heads, I went to his room; tails, I did not. It was tails. What about the girl? I flipped it again. It was tails again! What the hell? I walked lamely into the classroom and sat down next to the girl. Was she worth facing Mr. W.D.'s tyranny? Yessiree! The meeting was uneventful and after more of his jaw-jacking the class was dismissed. Mr. W.D. told me to stay.

"I ain't taking a whipping for being right," I mumbled to myself. The teacher passed me a photo album. My God! Mt. Zion Baptist Church on fire. The Dreamland Theater was in shambles. I was just there over the weekend. Whites with guns standing over dead bodies; Jeering white folks lining the streets as soldiers and vigilantes marched Blacks to concentration camps with hands held high, hats off and heads bowed. Trucks loaded with dead Blacks. Yellowing newspaper articles recounting block after block of destruction—"30, 75, even 300 dead" —just as he had described it.

"What you think, fat mouth?" he asked.

"I never knew ... nobody never told ... Big Mama, my mother, Floyd, or Auntie didn't ... Prof (Seymour Williams, my history teacher and no relation to Mr. W.D.) never said ... how could this happen?" It was one of the rare times when something other than loafing, mischief, and girls had seriously gained my attention. He was not passing a tale of a race war. It happened.

Mr. W.D. said white people wanted the valuable land in the Greenwood area for industrial purposes.

"Why didn't they just buy it?" I asked. "Even today most of the buildings are just old shacks."

He said Blacks wouldn't sell. Most of them had come to Tulsa with nothing but menial skills and determination. Blacks were out of slavery less than 60 years and owning land was the ultimate symbol of freedom.

"How did it get started? Why did Blacks take it? Why were they so silent?"

In answering my question, Mr. W.D. recounted the story of the elevator incident that the *Tulsa Tribune* reported as "an assault" on a white woman by a Black. The newspaper editorial in the *Tulsa Tribune* said to have incited the riot can't be found. It was clipped from all the copies of the newspaper, even in the archive at the Oklahoma Historical Society.

"Where are the pictures of Blacks fighting and the dead whites?" Mr. W.D. snarled back, "Peckerwoods took the pictures and sent them across the nation as postcards." The horrific photographs were a message from the Klan, aimed at intimidating Blacks and recruiting new members.

A warning came in 1912, when President Woodrow Wilson brought segregation back to Washington and reinvigorated racial separation across the land. The President endorsed D.W. Griffin's unambiguously racist movie, *The Birth of a Nation*, extolling the invisible empire. "It is like writing history with lightning," the president said. "My only regret is that it is all so terribly true." The 1915 film's debut was in the White House and the film revitalized the Ku Klux Klan in Oklahoma and the nation.

"Then, the Klan started the riot?" I asked Mr. W.D.

He said he thought the riot was more spontaneous than planned by the Klan or anybody. "So, if you're asking me was there a Klan meeting and a vote taken 'to lynch a nigger tonight,' I doubt it."

But then Mr. W.D. noted that all the big-shots downtown—the mayor, the police force, bankers, merchants, lawyers and hordes of bluebloods and rednecks—were Klan members and had designs on

Greenwood. The fat cats wanted this place. The rednecks wanted to keep Blacks in their place. Burning down Greenwood suited the purposes of both.

"Did you fight?"

"Yeap," he answered.

"Kill anybody?"

"That's enough. If you want to know more, talk to Mary Ann (Big Mama, my grandmother) and others in your neighborhood."

"Does Prof know about this?" Seymour "Prof" Williams was my history teacher. He taught what he called "the real history" but never mentioned the 1921 Race Riot and all those people killed. After a studied pause, Mr. W.D. answered, "This weekend we'll go by Seymour's house and you ask him."

Arriving home stunned and curious, I asked Mama about the riot. "I wasn't born yet," she answered. Maybe Big Mama knew. She never looked up from ironing, only ordered me to wash the dishes and study my learning.

Nonetheless, a chord of interest was struck in me. It surely started an imperceptible turning point for this never-do-well, disinterested youngster and set me on a path for a lasting solution against the contagion of racism.

The riot would influence my passion for civil rights and my advocacy against the war in Vietnam. It led me on the road to becoming a journalist, an Oklahoma lawmaker, and to an unshakable empathy for poor and disenfranchised people struggling up the mountain top.

7
Outgunned and Outlawed

The anger and frustration of the Black community is palpable and it's unlikely to subside anytime soon.
  Professor Charles Ogletree, Jr., Harvard University

IN AN EFFORT TO SATISFY my curiosity, I made my way eagerly toward Prof's home. It was one of the most memorable afternoons of my life.

When I arrived, Mr. W.D. was already there. Both men were anchored on the porch's double-seated swing slowly tossing themselves back and forth.

Prof greeted me angrily. "Boy, if you ever call me a liar, I'll beat you so badly they will have to bury you in pieces." Mr. W.D. had snitched on me. I was scared. Everybody knew Prof was crazy. The legendary football coach was a cross of Knute Rockne and Ivan the Terrible.

His stubby stature had bent with age, but the curve didn't disguise his athletic frame. When he spoke from the side of his mouth he exposed tobacco-stained squared teeth that appeared to be unevenly chopped from his biting on cigars. Prof's red suspenders pulled his baggy, wrinkled pants high above his waist. His white shirt showed evidence of the morning coffee and it was topped with a worn and once-red tie.

I never played hooky from Prof's class. I was afraid of him and that fear always led me into his classroom. "I like history," I told him. "I have never missed your class."

"As you know, I'd come down to that pool hall, snatch a knot on your head and drag you by your kinky hair all the way back to Booker T."

How did he know about my cutting classes for the pool hall? Time to move on.

I wanted to know about the Tulsa riot, why the community was silent, and why he had never mentioned the riot in class. This was odd in that Prof's unwritten syllabus was taught with his quarreling with history and the "lies." Prof's classes used torn, outdated books passed down from all-white Central High School's students, who got new and updated versions.

Prof made the pages of the past come alive, often correcting chapters from the secondhand books with "what really happened." He did not like white folks and this loathing for them was emphasized by his apparent anger. Prof held a special disdain for Thomas Jefferson, who he said spoke eloquently on the evils of "the peculiar institution," while rationalizing that his reason for owning slaves was debt. Jefferson said once the debt was cleared he planned to make his slaves "happy." Only his children by Sally Hemming, his slave mistress, were freed on his death.

During Jefferson's tenure as president, the U.S. purchased the 2 million-acre Louisiana Territory from France for $27 million. The land deal came as a direct result from the slave rebellion of Toussaint L'Ouverture in Haiti. Had it not been for the slaves' victory over Napoleon, the French wouldn't have been bankrupted.

The land sale doubled the size of the nation. It is ironic that the expansion of this slaveholding nation was due significantly to a slave revolt. Nearly 30 years later, peoples of the Five Civilized Tribes, and their Black subjects and Freedmen, would be forced onto these western lands. The tribes and the Blacks with them had become inconvenient for whites who confiscated the tribal land.

Prof surely believed that if somebody were to blame for the Tulsa Race Riot, it was Washington and the group that followed him with their idolatry for land and their moral collapse. His contempt in describing them introduced me to a new word: "bigot."

According to the old coach, Oklahoma had a "southern flavor of U.S. history." He said whites in Dixie are still fighting the Civil War. "If publishers wanted to sell their books down South, they had best tell the Dixie version: that Robert E. Lee was a gentleman drawn into the Confederacy to protect his Virginia homeland. That the Civil War was about states' rights. That the slaves were better off in bondage and a happy people. "Lies! All lies," he screamed.

"Robert E. Lee was a traitor," Prof declared, "and should have been hanged. The rich bastards of the South wanted the right to continue to work the shit out of slaves. The rednecks didn't want to lose their high sport of lynching."

He explained that for the North, the Civil War was no more than a real estate deal. Slaves were considered three-fifth human and their masters could count them in deciding the electoral politics of the land. Without the electoral count generated by slaves, Jefferson would have lost the 1800 presidential race to Adams and Andrew Jackson would have remained wandering in the backwoods of Tennessee.

When students' questions about his conflict with history agitated the cranky old professor, it evoked an angry response from him: "You're a dumb ass. I'm a warrior. I'm a Seminole."

Years later, his wife, "Miss Della," told me Prof was really part Cherokee. The coach hated how Cherokees had treated Blacks before and after the Trail of Tears. "The more profitable slavery became, the harsher and more brutal Cherokees treated Blacks," she explained, "so Seymour just changed tribes." In light of the Seminole Nation's attempts to oust Black tribal members more recently, today Prof might declare himself an Apache.

Prof was repeating diatribes about the "white man's evils" I had heard in class when I interrupted and asked about the riot and the silence that followed. The old man's answer could have been that offered by the French political historian Alexis de Tocqueville: "Once the majority has irrevocably decided a question, it is no longer discussed. This is because the majority is a power that does not respond well to criticism."

That isn't what he said, but surely what he meant when he told me, "These white men were the same trifling bastards and thieves who were chased out of England. Lying sons of bitches. Pocahontas should've let them starve."

Prof said while Negroes "didn't take no shit" and fought back, still they lost everything in the riot. Afterwards they were afraid another massacre could happen and there was no way to tell the story. The two Negro newspapers were destroyed. Disillusioned by unkept promises by white leaders to rebuild Greenwood, Blacks were too busy with improvisational survival and just trying to make it. Prof said Negroes didn't like to talk about the riot and so they didn't. "The killers were still running loose and wearing blue suits as well as Klan sheets."

During that time, working-class whites seeking opportunity could not win an election, or gain employment as a policeman or fireman, or work any other city job without Klan credentials. The rich and powerful were not only Klan members, they led the racist gang of bigots.

Why were Blacks quiet? "There were a lot of big-shot rednecks at that courthouse who ran the city and still do. In the aftermath of the riot, where could Blacks find justice? The police, the politicians, the National Guard, the Klan, even Jesus was white."

Mr. W.D.'s parents lost thousands of dollars in the destruction. He was the only child of John and Loula Williams, who owned the Dreamland Theatre, the first Black movie theater west of the Mississippi. They also operated movie theaters in Okmulgee and Muskogee. The Williams' theaters were hot spots on the Black entertainment's "chitterlin' circuit" for vaudeville shows, dance bands, and the latest movies. (The circuit was named for the "hog guts," a delicacy eaten by Blacks since slavery.)

The chitterlin' circuit rounded from Houston to Dallas, through Oklahoma City and Tulsa, from Omaha to Kansas City and all points in between. As a matter of fact, Count Basie was stranded in Tulsa when he linked up with the popular Oklahoma City-based Blue Devils, considered the best band on the circuit. Basie became a legendary musician and jazz icon. Many of the Blue Devils were members of the Count Basie Band.

Mr. W.D.'s parents also operated the East End Garage and Williams Confectionery and owned several rental properties. John and Loula Williams were among the richest Blacks in the state. They were the first in Greenwood to own an automobile. "A Norwalk," Mr. W.D. noted boastfully. It was stolen during the riot and never recovered.

After sporadic gunshots, early on June 1, 1921, a whistle blew. Mr. W.D. said airplanes were overhead, shooting and dropping fire bombs. Some of the buildings caught fire and the mob charged across the tracks. "My Dad said, 'Bill, get out of here.' I ran down the Midland Valley railroad tracks and was captured and marched to Convention Hall."

Both teachers insisted that Blacks were "winning the war" until the planes were dispatched to Greenwood. "We had the high ground," Mr. W.D. said. From their three-story building, the son loaded the rifles as the dad shot down on the mob. Blacks beat back rush after rush.

Imprisoned Blacks were required to wear name tags and be approved by a white person before their release. John Williams was hidden by a white man who worked at the Dreamland. The employee also vouched for the release of Mr. W.D. and his mother from the prison camp.

Despite their passion, Mr. W.D. and Prof admitted nobody really knows what happened. What they did know was Roy Belton, "a white man," was dragged from the same courthouse a year earlier and lynched as cops directed traffic. When Dick Rowland was arrested, word of his potential lynching spread quickly through Greenwood.

Earlier, on the evening of May 31, before the heavy fighting had broken out, Prof said he stood alone and armed to guard a light on Archer and Detroit near the center of the Black boulevard. "They were trying to sneak up on Greenwood from the west. When several of them approached the light, I made myself known. Each time they backed away." A World War I veteran, he said he was a "crack shot" and stayed at his post until firing ceased. "I went home, but they were not quitting. They were organizing."

Prof and his wife heard the loud whistle and saw the mob advancing to their place. "I got my pistol and was rushing to the door." He was tripped and his wife and a friend pounced on him, took the gun and threw it out the window. When the troopers came they said: "You got a gun boy'?"

With his head bowed, Prof said, "No."

The troopers placed them on a truck to a concentration camp.

"Sure as hell, if my wife hadn't taken my gun, they would have killed me, but I guarantee you, I would have taken a couple of them out." As they were leaving, Prof and his wife looked back to see their home burning.

Nearby, Mt. Zion Church was the scene of the most spectacular battles of the war. Fifty Blacks barricaded themselves in the church and refused to surrender. Three white men were killed as they advanced on the building. Machine guns were brought in by the National Guard. Many Blacks were killed in the attack. Trapped in the blazing church, the others surrendered. The fight was reported as having the heaviest casualties of any of the engagements. Police Major Charles W. Daley placed the toll of riot dead at 175. However, he said he believed a number of Negroes were burned to death when their homes were swept by fire.

Prof claimed Horace "Peg Leg" Taylor held his ground and is credited with single-handedly shooting dozens of white invaders.

In the years to come, I learned more details by talking with many people and extensive research. Lena Taylor Butler, Peg Leg's daughter, said her father sent the family down a ravine that led to the Midland Valley tracks and safety from the advancing mob. She was told her dad held off the mob until the airplanes began shooting down on him. She never heard from her father again and assumed he is among the unidentified dead buried in unknown places.

She said today, people see her father's story as heroic myth. "He is neither a myth or urban legend, but just one of the many who died in the riot attempting to protect his family, property, and community," she explained.

Adjutant General Charles F. Barrett, commander of the Oklahoma National Guard, on arriving on the scene with 109 soldiers, said whites were loading dead bodies of Blacks and removing them from the area.

He also noted all of the colored section appeared to be on fire and desultory firing continued between both sides. "Trucks loaded with scared and partially clothed Negro men and women were parading the streets under heavy armed guards," the adjutant general said. "In all my experience I have never witnessed such scenes that prevailed in this city when I arrived at the height of the rioting—25,000 whites armed to the teeth raiding the city in utter and ruthless defiance of every concept of law and righteousness."

B. F. Johnson, a Washington, D.C., publisher, was in Tulsa on a business trip and he saw the riot unfold from his hotel window. In his diary, Johnson wrote: "The white people were largely to blame—there seemed to be on the part of many white people a sort of joy in having unrestrained privilege of shooting the Negroes." From his account "probably 200" Blacks were killed. Johnson saw a Black man killed near the front entrance of the hotel.

Despite the gallant effort, Blacks were outgunned, outnumbered and outlawed. They were being fired upon by the white mob, vigilantes with law enforcement badges, the Tulsa National Guard, and at least two airplanes.

The *Wichita Daily Eagle* reported after the riot that a white man, Thomas Higgins, saw at least a dozen Blacks killed by law enforcement officers "while their hands were in the air."

The Revered R.A. Whittaker told the *Black Dispatch,* an Oklahoma City weekly, that hundreds of Black, men, and children are scattered through the bottoms of the Verdigris and Arkansas Rivers and pregnant women were seen fleeing from their homes as "bullets of the white assassins rushed them."

Tulsa police, sworn deputies, the local National Guard and vigilantes had become indistinguishable. The very fair-complexioned NAACP leader Walter F. White was deputized and infiltrated the mob. He reported for *The Nation Magazine* and declared "between 150 and 200 Negroes had been killed in the riots and at least 50 white persons."

The *Tulsa World* reported "One Negro was dragged behind an automobile with a rope around his neck." Decades later, former Mayor L.C. Clarke confirmed this report and Thelma Nelson, who married the brother of Mama's boyfriend Floyd, told me her mother had told her that an uncle was pulled behind a Model T, but his death was never reported.

The three-story Williams' Building was rebuilt in 1923 and appears little different from its predecessor. It is among the remnants

Pillage of Hope

that stand today as a memory of Black Wall Street. Mr. W.D. said his father was run out of Tennessee by whatever was chasing him and he came to the territory with nothing. A year after the riot, the Williams' three buildings, the Dreamland Theater and their garage were rebuilt, but their life savings were depleted.

There may have been thousands of marauding whites in the riot mob, but the aging militant coach implied that they all had one face, W. Tate Brady, one of Tulsa's most prominent citizens. Accused of inspiring the pillage, Brady offered $5,000 for anyone who could offer proof.

While there is little certainty of a linkage between Brady and the Klan to the 1921 Race War, afterwards there are reports that local public officials advised Klan leaders to avoid references to the riot, apparently to avoid drawing attention to the imprisoned, shameful, and homeless condition of African-Americans in Tulsa.

Brady was a wealthy and powerful member of the establishment. His political associations extended from City Hall to the governor's office and into the White House. In the aftermath of the violence, he was vilified by riot victims for fomenting the tragedy and for leading the conspiracy to steal their land through the infamous fire ordinance, which would have prevented Blacks from rebuilding by imposing requirements that buildings must be fireproof, made of concrete, brick or steel and two stories high. Ironically, Brady filed a lawsuit against insurance companies, for rental property destroyed during the race war, as did 179 Blacks. The court ruled against them all.

Brady's mansion stands today at 620 N. Denver, just blocks from the pillage. It's a replica of Robert E. Lee's Arlington, Virginia, home. The city father celebrated the rebel general's birthday annually with a ball, in full Confederate regalia. An incorporator of the City of Tulsa and one of its first aldermen, in 1903 Brady was the first to build a hotel in Tulsa, where Democrats headquartered and laid plans to control the Constitutional Convention leading to statehood and officially sanctioning segregation.

After the massacre, the Tulsa Chamber of Commerce formed a rebuilding committee. When a chorus of "No!" shouted down Mayor

T.D. Evans' nomination to it, the mayor dismissed the Chamber's committee and City Hall organized its own. Brady was appointed vice-chairman of the City's reconstruction committee, charged with rebuilding the charred, burned, and broken Black community. During a committee meeting he said, "We must never again allow the disgraceful shack town to be rebuilt in the old location—only again to be a hell hole.".

Brady ranted but offered no solution for housing the homeless as winter approached. The first and only action taken by the reconstruction committee was recommending to the City Commissioner and gaining approval of the infamous fire ordinance.

Brady maintained that they proposed the ordinance to conform to the white district across the tracks. Blacks could rebuild if they complied with the law and the hurdles it presented.

Mayor Evans, Brady's close friend and political ally, resisted building temporary housing. "These temporary houses, once erected, will be removed with difficulty," the mayor declared. "Let the Negro settlement be placed farther in the North and East," Mayor Evans said during the first meeting of the City Commission, after the riot. "A large portion of this district [Greenwood] is well suited for industrial purposes. We should immediately get in touch with the railroad with a view to establishing a union station on this ground."

Real estate agents and developers perused the fire-damaged area searching for quick profits. The City of Tulsa ran newspaper ads inviting wholesale houses, industrial plants and other businesses to consider Greenwood for investments. In 1921, Greenwood's business and residential community bordered on downtown and was on the doorstep of Tulsa's anticipated growth pattern.

The *Tulsa Tribune* solicited opinions from its readers in its *You Tell 'Em* column that asked: "What do you think of the proposal to create a new Negro district, reserving the south part of the burned area for a wholesale and industrial center?" According to the responses, the idea was "strongly favored," "splendid," "wonderful," "a good move," "the proper thing."

Oklahoma National Guard Adjutant General Charles Barrett ordered a moratorium on title transfers and halted the speculation.

The Oklahoma Klan was at its peak in the 1920s, virtually controlling state and many local governments. Two years after the riot, Governor J.C. Walton declared war on the hooded bigots.

He alleged that where the Ku Klux Klan operated most freely, "local officers were members of the Klan. A Klan sheriff made the arrest. A Klan county attorney prosecuted the charges against them in a Klan court before a Klan jury drawn by a Klan Jury Commission. Anybody opposed to them will be wading through a slaughter house into an open grave."

Governor Walton held that a state of "insurrection and rebellion" existed because of the Klan. The Governor placed the state under martial law and opened military tribunals against the hooded society. Compiled in the Walton papers at the University of Oklahoma, the transcripts of those tribunals are instructive.

According to the testimony, police who refused to join the KKK were fired, and there were "whipping squads" within the department. In a letter to the tribunal officials, Tulsa Attorney Robert J. Boone noted it was virtually impossible to gain a verdict against Klansmen. "The courts cannot properly function nor can anyone who doesn't belong to the Invisible Empire."

City leaders confessed that "Special Officers" were unpaid Klan members and routine volunteers who could only be appointed by the Police Chief or Police Commissioner. Former Mayor H.F. Newblock admitted to his KKK membership. Ironically, a park west of the city named for Newblock is thought to be a grave site for many of the unknown dead from the two-day holocaust.

Tate Brady told the tribunal that he quit the Klan because they attempted to tell him how to vote. "It was a disgrace to a man like my father," who he alleged was one of the Klan's original founders. However, he owned the building where the Klan was headquartered. Brady committed suicide in 1925. According to Prof his guilt about the riot was too much.

Governor Walton was impeached by the Oklahoma Legislature in part for his anti-Klan activities. State Senator Washington E. Hudson, a prominent Tulsa lawyer, was a founder and titular head of the Oklahoma KKK. He said bankers, businessmen and civic leaders were *all* members of the Klan. Indeed, records on file at the University of Tulsa support this claim. As Senate Majority Leader, Hudson led the fight to impeach Governor Walton.

It is very noteworthy that Dick Rowland, whose arrest for attempted rape triggered the riot, had all charges dropped against him.

After the 1921 Race War, there was a dramatic increase in KKK membership. In 1924, the Klan slate won all of Tulsa's municipal offices. Rebuilding the Black community and other issues left from the riot had been decided at the ballot box.

One of the great untold ironies of the riot is that there were many white businesses lost as well. Among the official records remaining from the conflict is a court record of a white businessman suing an insurance company for compensation. However, there was a riot exclusion in insurance policies written in the area and the court ruled against the victims. Despite the segregation, many white businesses on or near Greenwood catered to Negroes anyway.

I learned 35 years after the riot that nearly all the old folks in my neighborhood were riot survivors, including my Aunt Mildred, and that my grandfather's business had been destroyed. Over the years, I talked with many of them and read their comments in newspapers and other reports:

Jack Scott was a member of the courthouse convoy of World War I veterans. His daughter, Juanita Perry, was Mama's friend, and his son, Julius Scott, was our neighbor. Years later Julius and Juanita would offer their accounts to a commission studying the riot.

Augusta Mann said her brother-in-law, J.D. Mann, had led the group of veterans to the courthouse to stop the lynching.

George Monroe was under his bed when vigilantes came into his house and stepped on his finger. His sister placed her hand over his mouth to muffle the scream.

Clarence Fields was shooting from Standpipe Hill when airplanes fired and hit him on the hand. He proudly displayed his scar. "I got some good shots in," he said, smiling.

Dr. R.T. Bridgewater reported that a whistle blew, followed by shots from a machine gun located on Standpipe Hill. A cry was heard from a woman: "Open lookout for the airplanes. They are shooting upon us."

Mabel Little was attending services at Mount Zion Baptist Church when they were attacked. She escaped before the mob burned down the church. The building had just been dedicated a month before and its $85,000 mortgage was still due.

H.C. Whitlow lived on the west side in an apartment where the present City Hall is located downtown. "I saw a number of trucks pass our place loaded with dead bodies," he said. "I assume they were heading to the Arkansas River."

Joe Burns, said the riot was like World War I all over again "and our government did nothing to protect the innocent victims."

Otis G. Clark says some white mobsters were holed up in the upper floor of the Ray Rhee Flour Mill on East Archer. "They were just gunning down Black people and picking them off like swatting flies," he said. He never saw his stepfather after the riot. "He was a good family man. I know he did not desert us. He perished in the riot and all that burning."

Leroy L. Hatcher was nine days old when his mother ran to safety, dodging bullets with him in her arms. "The mobsters kicked in the door and set things on fire, my mother told me," Hatcher said. "My dad had told my mother to leave and he would be behind her. He never came. After the riot, she looked but never found him. His death haunted her for the rest of her life. I just wish I knew where they buried him and I could pay my respects."

Seven- year-old Ruth Avery, a white eyewitness, said she was riding the bus to school afterward and a truck passed filled with dead bodies. "The hand of a Black boy about my age was swinging back and forth over the side. His eyes were open and he looked like he had been scared to death." Avery said bombs were dropped from small airplanes. "They'd throw them down and it would burst into flames, setting buildings on fire." She later wrote a paper alleging an "official" report existed that placed the dead at 309. Many years later Mrs. Avery interviewed Fanny Brownlee Mish, who said her husband admitted to her that he drove a city-owned truck loaded with Black dead to an incinerator, where the bodies were dumped for burning. Mrs. Mish said she thought Blacks "deserved it."

James H. Goodwin was a very fair-skinned Black man and one of Greenwood's pioneering entrepreneurs. He had discovered the Promised Land in 1912 en route to Waterloo, Iowa, from his native Water Valley, Mississippi. When the riot came, Goodwin stood in front of his large house and directed the mob: "The niggers went that way." The Goodwin home was spared.

His son, Edwin L. Goodwin, Sr., was rounded up and slept on the ground for several days. Imprisoned Blacks were forced to wear ID badges and remained interned until a white person vouched for them. After the riot, the elder Goodwin came to the concentration camp and, assumed to be white, he collected his son.

There were exceptions to the cruelty. Some whites hid and protected survivors from the impending harm. Merrill and Ruth Phelps hid and fed Black victims in the basement of their home for days. Mary Erhard roomed at the downtown YMCA. She hid a Black porter who worked there. Renberg's Clothing Store offered clothes. The First Presbyterian and Holy Family churches opened their doors to fleeing refugees until they were taken to concentration camps. Sam Zarrow and his wife hid Blacks in the back room of their store.

Maurice Willows, the much respected and praised Red Cross director, was one of the very few candid white voices. He was the bridge between the Black refugees and white power structure. Historian Scott Ellsworth wrote that Willows' official report not only sheds light on one of the nation's darkest days, but tells the true story of courage and compassion in the face of overwhelming catastrophe.

Willows wrote to his Red Cross superiors: "All that fire, rifles, revolvers, shotguns, machine guns and organized inhumane passion could be done, with 35 city blocks with its 12,000 Negro population, was done. The number of dead is a matter of conjecture. Some estimates have the number of victims as high as 300, other estimates being as low as 55. The bodies were hurriedly rushed to burial and the records of many burials are not to be found." The Red Cross director advanced the idea that the riot was actually a well-planned plot. No criminal charges were made. No reparations followed this destruction of lives and property. No insurance claims were honored.

No lawsuits were won. The city council passed ordinances that made it very difficult for Black property owners to rebuild. The city council passed a fire ordinance, requiring fireproof building standards in the riot-damaged community, making it nearly impossible for Greenwood's citizens to afford to rebuild their businesses and homes. The political leaders decided no outside financial assistance would be accepted.

Attorneys B.C. Franklin, P.A. Chappelle, and I.H. Spears filed a lawsuit, *Joe Lockard v. City of Tulsa* and gained a temporary injunction against the fire ordinance. The city did not dispute the allegation of discrimination but protested that Lockard had not shown proof of illegality or injustice of the ordinance. A three-judge panel invalidated the proposed fire ordinance on a legal technicality—it had not been published a sufficient number of times. The city quickly passed a second ordinance and ordered it published.

Under the provisions of the new ordinance, the erection of frame buildings was forbidden and the ordinance was amended to include the northern half of the devastated area. Franklin told his clients to build with crates, build with boxes, "but build." A wealthy Greenwood entrepreneur told the *Chicago Defender*, "They had better have the jails ready for us because we are going to keep on building. Negroes are not waiting for winter to come and not have a place to live. They will carry their cases to the highest court in the land for redress."

One of the more strident voices against the fire ordinance was Mather M. Eakes. Eakes was an attorney and former judge, and chairman of the Tulsa County Commission on Interracial Cooperation. The interracial group was organized to improve social relations and halt lynching.

The former judge, representing the Rev. R.A. Whitaker, pastor of Mount Zion Baptist Church, and 12 other Black residents, called the fire ordinance unconstitutional, unjust, and oppressive and said its sole purpose was to remove Blacks from the Greenwood area to force the conversion into an industrial development.

Mary E. Seaman, the city auditor, testified that at the June 7, 1921, meeting of the City Commission, Mayor Evans discussed a resolution offered by the Tulsa Real Estate Exchange that the devastated area be made an industrial district, because it was ideally located and if placed in the fire district would lead to a substantial reduction of insurance rates throughout the city. The court found the fire ordinance unconstitutional.

Prof said that those who destroyed the Black community torched the soul of the city—an evil from which neither race has fully recovered.

"Why?" I asked.

"The Klan and fear was everywhere," Prof answered.

Prof's answer didn't satisfy me then or now. Black fear came after the riot. Before that, in his words, "They didn't take no shit." The Klan, at least the uninformed organized Klan, was less visible than marauding policemen, their deputies, and members of the Tulsa branch of the Oklahoma National Guard. Land speculators exploited the situation but couldn't have planned the Rowland incident that triggered the violence. Blacks had wealth, but the oil fields, though declining, still offered whites greater opportunities. Yellow journalism was a significant factor, but what was the mindset that could be further poisoned by journalists' racist words?

In 1917, with screaming headlines, the Tulsa press accused a Black man of assaulting a white woman. The police investigated and found he was framed by a wife cheating on her husband and the incident was cleared up without violence. So then, why the 1921 Tulsa race riot?

The completeness of the cover-up quieted any search for truth and many of the answers raise more questions. There were indisputably triggering influences, including the imposition of racial codes and segregation just after Blacks had fought for democracy in World War I. There was unionism that heightened suspicions of communist and socialist influences, race baiting by the Tulsa press, and the politically approved Klan infiltration of the police force. And I suspect that the very gall of armed Black veterans entering a white mob to prevent it from doing its will may have been among the factors that triggered the killing spree.

8
Blacks Instigate Riot?

War's always about land. From Alexander the Barbarian to these Klan-infested Niggah-hating Crackers. It was about land. They wanted Greenwood. They wanted Black-owned land.
                                             Professor Seymour Williams

O.W. GURLEY, Black Wall Street's founder, was a wealthy Arkansas entrepreneur. He bought 35 acres of land on the north side of Tulsa "to be sold to coloreds only." He apparently saw the segregated section as an urban evolution of all-Black towns and as an economic barrier against racism.

Perhaps Gurley's vision was to develop an area where doctors, lawyers, teachers, ministers, entrepreneurs, and other college-trained professionals could prosper in the larger city among their people, relieving them of the racism that rebuffed their services outside the Black community.

Gurley had resigned a presidential appointment in Arkansas and moved to the territory, first acquiring a homestead in Perry, Oklahoma. In 1905, he moved to Tulsa and opened a rooming house on a dusty trail he called "Greenwood Avenue," after an Arkansas town where he had once lived. Greenwood's first entrepreneur built his rooming house across the Frisco Railroad tracks on which many Blacks fleeing the South migrated to the Promised Land.

Gurley and his wife, Emma, also built three two-story buildings and five houses, and purchased an 89-acre farm in Rogers County. As their numbers grew, Blacks in Tulsa prospered. Whites bought adjoining land to exploit the pent-up market created by segregation.

Constrained by racism, Greenwood became one of the most successful Black business malls in America. According to the *Cincinnati Union*, on a visit to the area in 1913, the educator Booker T.

Washington told a gathering not to worry about being segregated, but to build up the section which had been assigned to them and they would make friends and become respected by the whites. Even though they were legally segregated and isolated by racism and social custom, the famed educator urged Blacks to "pull themselves up by their own bootstraps."

However, staying in their place and casting down their bucket where they were didn't appease whites nor stir the friendship Washington had forecasted. Whites of Tulsa were as committed to racism and segregation as they were devout in their faith in God. While Blacks suffered the venomous and shaming misery of being outcast, whites expressed their hostility with indifference, prejudice, or violence.

Dr. W.E.B. DuBois, an NAACP founder, was called a "race agitator" by Tulsa's white power structure. Dr. DuBois fiercely opposed Booker T. Washington's accommodation with whites. During a 1919 visit to Oklahoma, Dr. DuBois foretold Black Tulsa's reaction to an unfair dispensation of justice, such as the threatened lynching of Dick Rowland, and the resulting anti-Black terror: "When the murders come, he shall no longer strike us in the back. When the armed lynchers gather, we too must gather armed. When the mob moves, we propose to meet up with bricks and clubs and guns."

The DuBois visit was called one of the incendiary reasons for the warfare that would come. In 1919, across the nation, 30 Blacks were known to have been lynched and as many as 60 in 1920. In the decade preceding the Tulsa war, two women and 21 men were lynched in Oklahoma.

Gov. J.B.A. Robertson called an investigation of Dr. DuBois after the Tulsa riot. "If he is in any way responsible for this outrage, I'm going to have him indicted and tried as any other criminal should be," he said. Nothing came of the governor's promise.

There is little doubt that Greenwood's volatile, aggressive leadership reacted to whites' attacks on their rights. Cyril Briggs's Black Nationalist African Blood Brotherhood had an active chapter in Tulsa and vowed to stand up to the white man if attacked.

James Weldon Johnson, the executive secretary of the NAACP

and the author of "Life Every Voice and Sing," considered "the Negro National Anthem," said the riot was ignited because Tulsa Blacks "are probably the most prosperous and cultured body of Negroes in the country." He called the outbreak of violence in Tulsa "the worst of its kind that has happened in this country."

Richard Lloyd Jones was publisher of the *Tulsa Tribune*. His newspaper was accused of agitating the riot. In a column syndicated nationally, Jones called Blacks "beasts" and "dope fiends" and said that they held life lightly. "He is a bully and a brute," Jones wrote and said the riot was caused by "some loose mouth, shallow minded, blundering creature. 12 brutal Black men set out to shoot up the town." Agreeing with the NAACP leader, Jones judged the Tulsa riot the "worst race war in the history of the land."

On June 8, 1921, Victor F. Barnett, managing editor of the *Tulsa Tribune*, later announced that the publication had since learned that the accusations against Dick Rowland were untrue, including the story that the girl's face was scratched and her clothes torn.

In court testimony and in press accounts, Gurley named lawyer and hotel owner J.B. Stradford, *Tulsa Star* newspaper publisher A.J. Smitherman, and World War I veteran and storekeeper O.B. Mann as the leaders who inspired the outbreak of violence.

Gurley said the night of the riot he went to the *Tulsa Star* office at about 9 pm and found preparations already far advanced. "Guns and ammunition were being collected from every viable source." He said "many of the men were making open threats, talking in a most terrible manner and some were liquored up. ... When I saw what was going on, I tried to talk them out of this idea of arming themselves to prevent what they believed was a threatened lynching." Gurley told the court that Black leaders were "sending runners to part of the Negro section to round up there for us and to bring guns."

Gurley left the building when the 40 to 50 men threatened him and went to the courthouse to offer his assistance. Gurley said the real leader of the gang was Mann. He said Mann and his brother ran two or three stores in the colored quarters and stood well in the community. "This boy came back from France [as a World War I veteran] with exaggerated ideas about equality and thinking he could whip the world."

He said he didn't see Stradford or Smitherman at the courthouse, but Mann fired the first shot. He said the Negroes who were armed and marched on the courthouse started the trouble and the "good" colored citizens of Tulsa wanted them punished. "I personally lost property valued at $150,000 that I had labored a lifetime to accumulate," Gurley explained. "I am now an old man stricken with paralysis and my wife and I must face the future as best we can in our old age."

Gurley's testimony was given in a lawsuit demanding insurance companies pay for the properties lost in the riot. However, the insurance companies had a policy exemption against payment for properties "fired by riot," and the state Supreme Court ruled against the petition.

In his memoirs, lawyer B.C. Franklin said Gurley "exiled himself to California." Detested by Blacks and scorned by whites, the founder of America's Black Wall Street drifted into obscurity. Accused by Gurley of instigating the event that led to Greenwood's destruction, J.B. Stradford, A.J. Smitherman, O.B. Mann, and 57 others were indicted for inciting a riot. Stradford escaped to his brother's house in Kansas, where the governor refused to extradite him. Eventually, he was rescued from Kansas by his son and moved to Chicago.

John Baptiste Stradford was the son of a runaway slave whose father purchased his freedom and returned to Kentucky. A graduate of Oberlin College and the Indianapolis school of Law, J.B. settled in Tulsa, Indian territory, in 1899. He came to "the Promised Land" because of the successful establishment of all-Black towns and the possibility that Oklahoma could become a Black state. According to his memoirs, he was the first Black lawyer in the territory. In just a few years, he was known as one of the wealthiest entrepreneurs on the prosperous Greenwood Avenue.

On June 1, 1918, during an elaborate ceremony with bright lights glaring from the ornate chandeliers, the luxurious 65-room Stradford Hotel was opened at 301 N. Greenwood. According to Stradford it was the "largest and finest hotel in the U.S. owned and operated by one of our group." The hotel also held several other businesses.

Stradford had the reputation of not backing down from anyone,

Blacks Instigate Riot?

Black or white. On one occasion, a white deliveryman insulted the hotel owner's wife. The hot-blooded Stradford pistol-whipped him from his building and onto the street. Stradford warned the bleeding and battered man that if he returned to Greenwood, he would kill him.

The hotel owner's great-grandson, Chicago circuit Judge Cornelius Toole, said Stradford had the "courage and physical strength of a Mandingo warrior." In 1912, Stradford filed a lawsuit against the Midland Valley Railroad company, after he was removed from his luxury accommodations when the train reached the Oklahoma border. The lawsuit challenged Oklahoma's railroad segregation, protesting a violation of the Supreme Court's separate but equal mandate.

He held a first-class ticket and, in accordance with the *Plessy* decision, he contended that the Railway Company had to provide him first-class accommodation. The court ruled against the Greenwood entrepreneur but the case later became one of the stepping-stones for the Supreme Court decision in *Brown v. Topeka Board of Education*, which ordered the desegregation of public schools.

When the Tulsa City Commission passed an ordinance August 4, 1916, mandating segregation in neighborhoods and public accommodations, Stradford was a member of a committee that presented a petition to City Hall insisting the bill imputed a stigma upon the colored race ... and sapped the spirit of hope for justice before the law from the race itself. The Supreme Court overturned the ordinance; however, it was socially enforced until the Civil Rights Act of 1964.

In his memoir, Stradford insisted that he had no complicity in the riot. He said shortly after Dick Rowland's arrest, a meeting was held at the *Tulsa Star* office to decide what to do. Stradford, Smitherman, and a number of World War I veterans were present. By the hotel owner's account, the *Tulsa Tribune* headline alleging the rape of a white woman in an elevator by a Black man "aroused the wrath of the Ku Klux Klan and a white mob gathered at the courthouse." There was lynching talk.

Sheriff Willard McCullough telephoned Stradford and said the boy was safe and if he needed help he would call. Still, Stradford vowed to go to the courthouse single-handed to resist the lynch mob. However, he said the group thought if they were arrested, Stradford was more valuable as a lawyer to assist them from the outside.

Smitherman elected to take Stradford's place in the armed caravan to the courthouse. They found "at least 5,000 whites" demanding the sheriff turn over the accused man. According to Stradford, a white police officer attempted to take the gun from one of the veterans. "Our boys shot into the crowd and a number were killed and wounded and not since the Civil War had such violence been witnessed on American soil."

In the midst of the riot, Stradford was driven to the convention hall by the troopers and was told by a deputy sheriff that 150 men were lying dead on the streets. Three years to the day it opened, Stradford Hotel and his other properties were reduced to rubble.

His escape to Kansas is filled with intrigue. He remained a fugitive, living in Chicago, until his death at 75 in 1935. He never returned to Tulsa and never forgot his loss, or his humiliation, according to Judge Toole. Stradford's descendants are among the Windy City's most prominent citizens and made several attempts to clear his name.

In 1995, Judge Toole contacted my state legislative office about clearing his grandfather's name. I convinced Gov. Frank Keating to posthumously pardon Stradford. The governor formally apologized to Stradford's descendants, many of whom were present during ceremonies at the Greenwood Cultural Center, across the street from where the hotel once stood. In his remarks, the governor said: "The great tragedy and the hatred removed the talent of Stradford and his descendants from Oklahoma."

A.J. SMITHERMAN SHAPED THE SPIRIT of Black Wall Street, as an influential leader and the conscience of Tulsa's Black community. Smitherman was born in Childersberg, Alabama, in 1883. After graduating from Northwestern University, he founded the *Tulsa Star*. The outspoken editor maintained a continuous and fearless denunciation against Jim Crow and urged his community to stand firm against racial inequality. Smitherman maintained an ongoing accounting of the victims of lynchings, or near-lynchings, in the *Tulsa Star*. The white newspapers, albeit for different reasons and for different reactions, also printed lynching numbers.

In 1917, in Dewey, Oklahoma, less than 50 miles north of Tulsa, the Black community was destroyed by a white mob. According to records from the NAACP's national headquarters, N. Widlow was accused of killing the police chief and seriously wounding the city clerk. After Widlow was captured and shot, the *Tulsa Star* reported "the mob, enraged at being cheated of its victim," destroyed 200 homes, two churches, and a school.

Smitherman researched the incident and sent a report to the governor, resulting in the arrest of 36 men, including the town's mayor. In an editorial comment he wrote: "The *Tulsa Star* is unalterably opposed to mob violence, regardless of the color of the men composing it. We have had some actual experiences with the cowards who compose mobs, which have convinced us that two or three determined men armed for the occasion can thwart the purpose if they act in earnest and in time."

In 1917, Smitherman sided with Black hotel porter Jimmy Nichols, falsely accused of attacking a white woman. The publisher accused the *Tulsa Evening World Sun* of sensationalizing the case, claiming in bold headlines that the "plucky white woman" had received bruises on her breast and hip, and her fingers were bitten off while fighting off the porter.

The hotel's owner reported a different version to the police and Nichols was released. An investigation found the married woman was beaten by her Indian boyfriend. Smitherman noted such newspaper stories had been the direct cause of many innocent Negroes being lynched.

Lynchings documented in the Smitherman's paper included these:

In Okemah, an innocent Black man accused of murder and robbery had been pulled from the jail. His mother was seized from her home and she and her son were lynched from a bridge spanning the Canadian River while hundreds of whites watched.

In Wewoka, a Black man was strung up in front of the courthouse. The authorities didn't bother to investigate the lynching.

One hundred white men stormed the jail in Wagoner County and lynched a Black prostitute for killing a white man who had refused to pay for her favors. Commenting on the Wagoner murder, the *Daily Oklahoman* editorialized: "The conclusion is inescapable that we indulge in lynching so often because, as a race, we thirst for Negro blood, and love the excitement which attends the stringing up of a Black man."

Smitherman and other Greenwood leaders joined Black farmers and local police in Bristow as a protective wall against a mob's intent to lynch Black men falsely accused of raping white women.

In 1920, Smitherman protested to the governor about the Tulsa lynching of Tom Owens, a young white man. Gov. J.B.A. Robertson called on the publisher to assist with the investigation.

On January 4, 1921, in a message to the legislature, Gov. Robertson observed that lynchings were permitted to occur in Tulsa and Oklahoma City, not only with the tacit understanding of the sheriffs in those two counties, but made possible "by and through the connivance and participation of officers." The governor said evidence was destroyed or covered up, and alibis manufactured for the purpose of preventing the prosecution of law enforcement officials.

After a mob, aided by police officers, pulled a Black man from an Oklahoma City jail and lynched him, Smitherman noted that if any such attempt was brought to Tulsa "blood would pave the streets." His prophecy became Tulsa's reality.

In the 1921 riot, Smitherman lost a press valued at $4,000 and his home. The editor was forced into exile with his wife and five children. On the run and penniless, he fled to Boston and then Springfield, Massachusetts. In 1926 he settled in Buffalo, New York, where he started another newspaper. Later he served as President of the Associated Negro Press for 11 years. From his distant post, he published several poems about the "Tulsa Martyrs" and sent dispatches about the atrocities throughout Black America. While escaping Tulsa justice, Smitherman poetically described the riot from his distant corner:

Blacks Instigate Riot?

Think He Can Whip the World;
Greenwood Veterans Confront the Mob
Thus responding to their duty,
like true soldiers that they were,
Black men face the lawless white men,
under duties urgent spirit.

Cries of "let us have the nigger"
"lynch him, kill him," came the shout.
And at once there came the answer
when a sharp report rang out.

Stand back men, there will be no lynching
Black men cried and not in fun
bang! bang! bang! Three quick shots followed,
in the battle had begun
in the fusillade that followed
four white lynchers kissed the dust
many more fell badly wounded,
victims of their hellish lust.

Smitherman died in 1961 in Buffalo and his obituary was duly noted in the *New York Times*. He was 76.

Gurley, in his court testimony, falsely accused Stradford, Smitherman, and O.B. Mann as the riot ringleaders, but he furthered his mistake by naming the wrong Mann brother. The Mann brothers were prosperous neighborhood grocers, known by their initials: J.D., O.B., M.M., A.J., and P.P. Mann. It actually J.D. who was in the meeting at the *Tulsa Star*'s offices and led the gang to the courthouse. According to a nephew, John Mann, stories from his elders insist that when the melee erupted at the courthouse, O.B. Mann was en route to the bank with a "a pillowcase full of money," and had to shoot his way back home. "He was never at the courthouse," the nephew asserted. He said his uncle O.B. was protecting his life and his money. O.B.'s finger was shot off and he killed several whites as he was chased back to Greenwood, John Mann said.

Pillage of Hope

J.D. Mann was active in World War I veteran organizations. When word came of the impending lynching of Dick Rowland, J.D. Mann, Ed Howard, Jack Scott, and other former soldiers armed themselves and headed to the jail to determine the man's safety for themselves. Barney Cleaver, a Black deputy sheriff, assured the Greenwood troopers that everything was under control and ordered them to return home. They left.

As rumors and newspaper stories circulated, the courthouse mob swelled. Fearing a lynching, about 25 Black men returned to the courthouse where 5,000 or more whites were already gathered. Officer John McQueen advanced to take a gun from Johnny Cody. A shot was fired and then several more. William Daggs, a white local manager of Pierce Oil Company, fell dead. Cody was wounded and, while surrounded by the mob, he was left to bleed to death. Separated from their accomplices, Ed Howard and John Wheeler were later found dead. Mann, Scott and the others reached the corridors of Greenwood.

Gurley fingered O.B. Mann as one of the instigators. It was actually his brother J.D. who was in the meeting at the Tulsa Star's offices and led the game to the courthouse. According to a nephew, John Mann, stories from his elders insist that when the melee erupted at the courthouse, O.B. Mann was en route to the bank with "a pillowcase full of money," and had to shoot his way back home. "He was never at the courthouse," the nephew asserted. He said his uncle O.B. was protecting his life and his money. John Mann said O.B.'s finger was shot on and he killed several whites as he was chased back in Greenwood.

J.D. Mann escaped on the Midland Valley Railroad track caravan and, with hundreds of other refugees, he fled to Claremore and safety. Later, he opened a market at 902 N. Greenwood, and retired after an urban renewal program purchased and demolished the building in the 1970s.

After the riot, O.B. Mann escaped to Canada. The family sent him money and later he quietly and uneventfully returned home. The Mann Brothers' store on Lansing Avenue, owned by O.B. and his brother M.M., was outside the firewall and untouched by the riot.

Blacks Instigate Riot?

On December 11, 2007, 12 years after Stradford was pardoned, unsubstantiated charges of inciting the Tulsa race riot were dismissed against Smitherman, O.B. Mann, and 52 others. The injustice was discovered, researched, and pursued by Dr. Barbara Nevergold of the University of Buffalo while researching the life of Smitherman, who had escaped to Buffalo with his wife and five kids.

Not one person of the 10,000 or more who attacked the Black community was indicted. What is surprising is that the list of indicted Black residents includes Horace "Peg Leg" Taylor and several others who were said to have been killed in the early hours of the riot. The indictment petition is the only time the near-mythical figure's name has been listed in any official riot documents.

Also listed in the indictment was Johnny Cole (listed as Johnny Coley) who was shot, surrounded by the mob, and left to bleed to death as the first Black casualty of the race war. Others indicted by the grand jury but listed among the dead were Charlie "Commodore" Knox, Ed Howard, Ed locket, Curly Walker and Andy Brown. Knox's daughter Arlene was a friend whom I met during the Tulsa Civil Rights Movement.

J.H. Smitherman, the brother of A.J. Smitherman, remained in Tulsa despite the indictment and became a police officer. A few years later he was kidnapped by the Ku Klux Klan and had an ear cut off. Jack Scott ignored the indictment and was never arrested and remained active in the black community. His son Julius was a neighbor and his daughter Juanita was a close friend of my Mama.

9
The 60's

Segregation is the adultery of an illicit intercourse between injustice and immorality.
Dr. Martin Luther King, Jr.

My youthful excursion into the intrigue of the riot ended as I prepared to graduate from high school. There was a problem. I was called into the principal's office and warned that I had flunked the required vocational education classes and would likely return the next year. It seems the school had a silly rule that male graduates were required to pass a trade class. It could be carpentry, auto mechanics or tailoring. In my sophomore year, I selected carpentry. I flunked. The next year, I failed auto mechanics. In my senior year, I was no more remarkable in tailoring. I always placed shop in the last hour of my schedule and left the school grounds for the Big Ten Pool Hall. When principal H.C. Whitlow called me into his office, he complained that I had only reported to shop three times during the year. I was not surprised or bothered.

"Boy! I don't know what you could be," he chided.

Mr. Whitlow said completing my assignment and passing the tailoring class was my only chance of graduating. I told him I had nothing else to do and didn't mind returning the next year.

"Sit. Stay here," he shouted. After the principal left the room, I placed his pack of Camel cigarettes in my pocket.

He returned with the tailoring instructor, ordering him to "get this dummy out of my school. I don't care how you do it. I want him gone." "Big" Ben McKinney, the 400-pound tailoring instructor, had two classmates complete my assignment and passed me with a D-. Assured of graduating, I was ready for higher education and returned to the pool hall.

After graduation, many of my friends entered college or married. Neither of those options excited me. I quit my job washing dishes and turned full-time pool shark, placing my proficiency against the more-skilled players. That proved not to be a promising career.

Broke most of the time, I was pressed by Mama to "do something or get out." She grumbled about my sleeping late and pigging out on the groceries. The few classmates still available for loafing had the same problem. One afternoon, five of us decided to join the Air Force. I wanted to fly airplanes. We were told to return to the recruiting office the next day for testing. I was the only one who showed up.

The committee said I would make a good pilot. Teachers had always told me I was smart, but lazy. The multiple-choice questions were easy enough but boring. After about 50 minutes I started punching the testing cards randomly. I finished while the other recruits were still working on their answers. I was on my way to my pilot's wings and would leave for basic training in a week.

The week passed soon enough. I was only Black on the bus that rambled from Tulsa to Oklahoma City. After a physical, we were ushered back onto a bus where I expectantly proceeded to the back seats. The bus stopped at the Skirvin Hotel. As I attempted to exit with the white boys, a sergeant rudely shouted, "Sit down, boy!"

The bus scooted to a stop at the Oklahoma City YMCA for Blacks. The sergeant handed me a voucher for a room and a meal ticket. I would be picked up at 0800 hours the next morning and travel to San Antonio, Texas, for basic training. A nice lady greeted me and showed me my room.

I returned to the lobby, where I had seen a pool table.

"Want to play," Willie Moon asked.

I said, "Yes."

He said, "How much?" I had a dime and the meal ticket, which could be redeemed at a nearby restaurant. He won both.

"You hungry?" he asked, and fed me with my voucher.

That evening Willie took me to a party. When the girls learned I was to become a pilot, I left with a pocket filled with phone numbers and a heavy-set girl took me to her home. Her parents were gone. She offered me passion and intimacy. I promised to write and promptly forgot her name.

I saw Willie years later and we recalled the event. As it turned out, the pool shark had no money that day and planned to run out the door had he lost. When I think of my first erotic adventure, I owed Willie one big girl.

The next morning the bus headed for San Antonio. I retired to my backseat alone as the white youngsters talked and laughed together. Nobody said anything to me the entire trip. When the bus stopped to eat, I was told to wait as others entered the segregated café. The sergeant returned and handed me a box lunch.

On arriving at training camp, we were assigned a troop and barracks. Nearly half of the recruits were Black and close to even between northerners and southerners. I had not spoken for hours and was happy to see my own people. I made a point of meeting each of them and talked and talked and talked, until one of them nicknamed me Gabby. After a couple of days, the training inspector said we were to elect a barracks chief.

"How about Gabby," Claudale Huey, a muscular Black from San Francisco shouted.

"Yeah!" was the united response.

The white guys appeared intimidated by the Black solidarity. There were no other nominations. I had won my first political election and this experience led to my first encounter with Black consciousness.

The following day I was told by the training inspector to take a vote and name the flight. There were two final nominations, "The Yankee Clippers" from the northern wing and the "The Dixie Rebels" from the south. The vote was a tie with one vote left. Mine.

My brainwashing suggested that Confederate Gen. Robert E. Lee and his boys were just protecting their property from Yankee intruders. It didn't occur to me that my ancestors were their property.

I raised my fist and shouted, "We're the Dixie Rebels."

Southern boys broke out in song: *"I wish I was in the land of cotton, old times there are not forgotten."* The Southerners pointed to me and a loud baritone voice, I screamed: *"in Dixie land, I'll take my stand to live and die in Dixie!"*

I was stunned when the yells carried as many boos as cheers. The next few days, whites were friendly and Blacks appeared to have chilled toward me. On Saturday night, the United Service Organization hosted a dance at Arnold Hall. Shortly after my arrival, Claudale Huey, the muscle-bound Black who had nominated me as barracks chief told me to step aside. I was pleased. The silence was broken.

He led me to the dark side of the building and began pushing me in the chest. "Why are you siding with them crackers?" he screamed over and over as he continued to push me in the chest. "You ain't nothing but a Black redneck."

Obviously, he didn't realize I was a battle-tested bully. I put up my dukes. My defense didn't hold off his pop to my top lip. Blood spattered everywhere. I still carry a hickey on my upper lip from that left hook. The next morning, I stood for reveille with my lips swollen. The instructor asked me what happened and I said I fell. There was a muffled laughter among the recruits.

Afterwards, Huey thanked me for not snitching on him. "This is my only chance," he said. "There is nothing for me back home."

Until he busted me in the mouth, I had not recognized how easily I accepted racism. I was now a changed man and a solid "Negro." We became friends and remained so throughout our Air Force career. He was the best man when I married.

That was not the last bad experience I had in basic training. The only gun I had ever fired was a pistol. On our first trip to the rifle range, we were told to lie in a prone position. The trainer explained the procedure. We were to load an empty cartridge, aim at the target and practice "squeezing the trigger." I was gabbing and didn't hear all the instructions. On command, I inserted a *loaded* cartridge into the rifle.

The trainer stood before me with legs apart and asked, "Can you see the target under my nuts?"

I screamed, "Yes, sir!"

"Aim and squeeze the trigger."

I shook my head back and forth and hollered, "No, sir!"

"Boy, look under my nuts, find the target, and squeeze the trigger."

"No, sir!"

The 60's

"Do you want your ass kicked all over this range?"

"No, sir!"

"Then aim and squeeze the trigger."

Sweating profusely, I shut my eyes and fired the gun. Dirt kicked up in front of the instructor and he must've jumped a full 13 feet into the air.

"You Black son of a bitch. Get your ass out of here."

As I ran, he was throwing rocks at me and, in exceedingly bad taste, he used the N-word and other expletives as I raced away from him. For the rest of basic training, rather than return to the rifle range again, I reported to mess hall and peeled potatoes.

There was a brighter side. Word of my missed shot traveled throughout the base. Even the white boys treasured my assassination attempt of the terrifying trainer.

Graduation and flight school was nearing. I received the outstanding leadership certificate. A smart and confirmed military leader, I would now fly planes. We were told to report to the administration for assignment.

Some guys were worried about what job they would be assigned and where they would be stationed. Not me. Any hidden fears were reduced when I faced my assignment administrator. He was Black and friendly.

I told him what career I was promised by the recruiter. He read my records, frowned, and then went through them again.

"What planes will I be trained to fly?" I asked.

He said nothing. His lengthy review was only interrupted by a "hmmm" and then by more "umm, humm." He then looked up and said, "We got it."

"Where will I be stationed?"

"Clovis, New Mexico. "

"What planes are there?"

"The F-15."

"Are they fighters, or bombers?"

"Fighters."

"Whoopee!"

Then, rather sternly he explained: "Airman, you may become a good pilot one day, but right now Air Force needs come first and what we need is cooks."

"You say what? But I was promised ..."

He stood, offered me a salute, and said, "Next!"

Despondent, I returned to the barracks to gather my things. As we said goodbye, the inevitable question was asked: "Gabby what did you get?"

I started to lie—I can lie when the truth will do—but instead I bowed my head and said, "I'm a cook."

There was a chorus from the Black guys—four, six, twelve or more said, "Me, too!"

The white boys seemed happy with their assignments. Even the four-eyed misfit white boy from Iowa who liked to hang with the Blacks would become the weather forecaster as he was promised.

I have rarely set high goals for myself, and when good things don't pan out, I place them under the category of "shit happens" and move on. Even today, my friends tell me I'm a great cook. I was to be stationed with the buddy who had bloodied my lip. In Clovis, New Mexico, we were inseparable.

The small town was awful. However, had I not been stationed at Clovis, I would never have met my wife. We are the parents of six wonderful children: Kavin, Edward, Reginald, Ronald, Curtis, and Donna. Curtis died in 1994 from diabetes.

Meeting my future wife was accidental. I was 19 years old at the time, with a forged identification card that allowed me to enter the adult "Joy Club" where booze was sold illegally. Most of the underage GIs spent their free time at the boogie banging hut across the street, dancing to the rhythms of Ike and Tina Turner and other R&B entertainers of the day.

One weekend when the Joy Club had been raided and closed, I swaggered over to the teenagers' joint. It was packed with girls, heavily guarded by the civilian boys who lived to violently stifle any romantic contact between the local girls and airmen. Armed with a bottle of whiskey, I lured some of the gangbangers outside for a nip of "good scotch." I was now considered one of their "homies" and they allowed me to dance with the girls without combat.

The 60's

I reached for the hand of the girl standing next to me and she brandished a shy smile that lit the dim hut. She was gorgeous with striking features. Her hair was bundled in the back and stretched across a wide forehead above long, heavy eyebrows and large brown eyes. I gazed across the length of her shapely frame, an approving, even lustful, assessment. Her breasts pushed boastfully from her blouse and rounded perfectly below her neck.

The conversation in the club seemed to hush for our meeting and then became a symphony of musical noise. James Brown, The Godfather of Soul, shouted his trademark scream. The two of us broke into the "Mashed Potato," the latest dance craze.

The mahogany-complexioned princess weaved and whirled with the eloquence of a self-taught ballet dancer, mesmerizing her prince. She was sensational, twisting through the Mashed Potato's pirouettes. Whatever "it" was, this Princess had it.

After the dance, I did something flirty and offered to walk her home. She said something back. I wasn't listening. I'm accustomed to rejection. Then she repeated it. "I'm ready." The boogie-woogie gods were smiling on me.

The next morning, half asleep and barely sober, I convinced myself she was in the barracks with me, holding me and whispering softly and sexily. Allowing me to embrace her in an enchanted expression of passion. Love! This is love.

"Wake up! Say something sweet to her," I pressed myself. I finally opened my eyes. It was all a dream. I was alone. I staggered to the bathroom, looked in the mirror, smiled, and then cleaned away the devil-red lipstick smeared across my lips.

Frank Sinatra's ballad explained my feelings best:
she takes the winter
and makes it summer ...
Summer could take
some lessons from her ...

Princess D, my 18-year-old regal beauty, Diane Dawson, and I were married four months later. At family gatherings and during holidays, I've often teased that if Diane had been standing across the room, I would have met and married somebody near me or finished my scotch, got drunk, and returned to the base a single man.

Her version is that I cut in on a dance, and for the rest of the night and the next two weeks or more begged to take her to a movie until she felt sorry for me and said yes. Diane's account is closer to the truth, but why mess up a good story.

In the Air Force I had paid little attention to the Civil Rights Movement until Memorial Day 1961. After the parade on a hot afternoon, airmen lined up for a Pepsi or more in the Busy Bee Restaurant. After an hour or so, virtually everybody except the Blacks had been served. After noisy complaints, the waitress said the restaurant didn't serve Negroes.

I joked: "I don't eat em. Give me a hamburger." Nobody left.

Huey was angry. "I'm from California," he shouted. "We don't take this shit."

I suggested that we go to the soul food joint nearby.

"No way!" he barked.

In Oklahoma we were accustomed to taking shit and you get over it.

Huey stood on a table and began shouting about the injustice. "We are prepared to die for you and we can't buy a Pepsi?"

I was thinking, "Why is he making trouble?" We didn't like hillbilly music and I didn't see any hot sauce on the tables. Louisiana Hot Sauce is the spice Blacks require on all food.

A near-riot ensued as Blacks pounded on the tables and hollered obscenities. The Air Force police were called.

There are only two words in the English language that accurately describe when you can't lie out of trouble: "Oh! Oh!" We were carted off by the Air Force police for this "Oh! Oh!" moment and confined indefinitely to the base. It was reported in *Jet* magazine as the first civil rights demonstration in the Armed Forces.

My arrest was less about civil rights and more about not finding a back door. No charges were filed and the restrictions were never lifted. For the rest of our tenure in New Mexico, off-duty Blacks involved in the melee had to slip into town.

After the arrest, more Black GIs began paying attention to Dr. Martin Luther King, Jr.'s nonviolent confrontation with segregation.

We ranked a state's degree of racism by the news reports on civil rights demonstrations. There were no reports of such activity in Oklahoma, so my state was placed in the category of "Black friendly." I neglected telling my buddies that in 1958, a contemporary of mine, 16-year-old Barbara Posey, led one of the first protests in the nation, which without press attention went ignored. Later, Claire Luper had led the Oklahoma City NAACP's youth chapter in some of the earliest sit-ins in the nation, but they had gone unreported nationally.

I ignored Oklahoma history. I had forgotten the 1921 race riot—but not for long. After a reluctant beginning, upon my discharge from the Air Force, I by chance became a civil rights activist.

In 1963, the Civil Rights Movement came to Tulsa. The young militants of the day were stymied at first because the NAACP was controlled by the elders of the Black community who wanted no troubles.

The old folks had survived the riot and warned that militant behavior could break the calm and instigate creeping episodes of race hatred. The emerging young leaders opened a chapter of the Congress of Racial Equality (CORE) and began picketing restaurants. Ironically, CORE's first fundraising event, featuring comedian Dick Gregory, was held at the segregated Tulsa Club that could be rented for all-Black events.

At first, I thought CORE people were crazy. Recently discharged from the Armed Forces, I prided myself in being "too violent" for the movement. More than a bit cowardly, I bragged about being a follower of Malcolm X. I liked Malcolm but thought the Muslims really went too far, calling for what I thought was a separate economy.

Malcolm X preached that Blacks should defend themselves against whites' violence. I thought, "Right on!" Still, I was also afraid of losing what I had. I drove a new white Fairlane 500 Ford and held a good job as the state's first Black baker in a union shop. I lived in a house on a shady street where whites were steadily evacuating. I had a wife and three kids now.

Life was good.

One morning I drove to Eaton's Barbershop, the launching place for the civil rights demonstrations. I was asked to drive the demonstrators to Borden Cafeteria, deep in the white area. I refused at least four times. Finally, I was coaxed into driving them. Civil rights demonstrators would be arrested, packed into paddy wagons by police, and would go right back to the picket lines. At a safe distance, I watched and waited 10, 20, 45 minutes for the cops. Nothing happened. I became concerned. I tiptoed to the door and stepped in.

Just before my entrance, the owner had changed his mind about leaving the loudly singing demonstrators lingering in line. He escorted whites around them and finally called the cops. The door opened behind me and the police and media stormed in.

The last to enter, I was the first arrested. Waving a clenched fist, I was packed out screaming, "I'm not with them. This is a mistake. I'm innocent!"

My fear was reported as anger in the evening news headlines: "Protesters arrested."

En route to jail, the militants sang.

I cried. "My life is over," I thought.

CORE lawyers were waiting at the jail to bail us out. Two hours late to work, I knew I would be fired at the Wonder Bread bakery where I had integrated the workforce. I would lose my house, my car, and my good life.

In the nine months on the job as the bakery's only Black worker, not one of the white coworkers had spoken to me. On this day, Tom Sullivent patted me on the back and told me to stand up for my rights. We remain friends to this day.

Kenny Ruth, the union shop steward, told me if any foreman jumped me to call him. "As long as you do your job, they can't mess with you." This was a seminal moment in my life.

I realized that nonviolence was courageous and my claim of being too violent was really a phobic fear of white people. I became active in the labor union, earning the friendship of most of its members. Before I quit the bakery to become another "first Black" in a non-traditional job at American Airlines, I declined support from union members to become its business agent. Had I taken that job, I would have become the first Black in the nation to head a majority white union. At the time, another guy and I were the only Blacks in the union.

I joined CORE's most militant faction. The civil rights group was picketing North Side State Bank, where most Tulsa Blacks held their accounts, yet even the janitors were white. While I was negotiating with the bank's president, he asked me how many jobs we were demanding. I quipped, "One! If it is the president." The banker hired a cashier and a janitor, and placed a Black minister, the Rev. T. Oscar Chappelle, on his Board of Directors. Rev. Chappelle became a very close friend and mentor who rescued me from self-inflicted messes more than once.

A "whites only" wash house bordering on the Black community was a CORE target. The owner stood at the door and would only allow whites to enter. I pulled the white boy from our ranks and he held the door open as we crowded into the laundry for the nation's first "wash-in." The owner said he had a heart condition and pleaded with us to leave, that the stress might kill him. I advised the bigot that in his case racism was an occupational risk and a hazard to his health. The expression on his face revealed an enlightened experience. The segregationist had finally surrendered to the notion that he could no longer hold onto a bygone day. Weeks later he sold the business to a Black.

There is one crazy thing from this period that I file under the category of "what were you thinking?" In 1964, Tulsa's CORE chapter collected canned goods for Freedom Summer, an effort in which all the civil rights organizations had converged on Mississippi for a voter registration campaign. There was a call for volunteers to drive a truck filled with canned goods from Tulsa to feed the workers in the Mississippi campaign. I joined the crew with another Black man and a white girl. We were to drive 500 miles through the dark roads of Arkansas into Mississippi. The entire route was a likely place for lynching. We stopped at gas stations and defiantly used the bathrooms. All the bearded, stereotypically hillbilly attendants were courteous.

We arrived in Clarksdale, Mississippi, and left without incident. What scares me today is that fear never approached me. A few weeks later, fellow CORE members James Chaney, Michael Schwerner, and

Andrew Goodman, also in Mississippi for the Freedom Summer, were murdered in Philadelphia, Mississippi, on a similar dark and lonely road just a three-hour drive away. We were a redneck, racist sheriff away from becoming martyrs.

After the murders, a second CORE truck was stopped in Arkansas. The volunteers told the cops what they were doing and were escorted to the Mississippi state line. Years later, my friends on that trip told me they too were not afraid "even when stopped by the police." Al Hill (older brother of Anita Hill, who testified against the Supreme Court confirmation of Clarence Thomas), one of the founders of the Tulsa CORE chapter, declared: "I guess we really meant it when we said we were willing to die for our rights."

CORE continued to picket for public accommodation, jobs, housing, and social decency, as Tulsa resisted. Dr. King pricked the conscience of the nation with his "I have a dream" speech and, in doing so, forced President John F. Kennedy to propose the Civil Rights Act. President Lyndon B. Johnson signed the bill into law. The U.S. Supreme Court declared "one man, one vote" in 1964 and ended years of disenfranchisement of Black voters and city dwellers.

A Tulsa legislative district was reapportioned to include most of the Black community. Even though Blacks were still a minority in numbers, the area was in racial transition and whites were on the run. Curtis Lawson launched a campaign to become the first Black person elected to the Oklahoma state legislature since 1908. James Goodwin, son of the *Oklahoma Eagle* publisher and grandson of the Greenwood pioneer J.H. Goodwin, was chairman, and I served as campaign manager. Three other Blacks were elected to the state legislature from Oklahoma City. The campaign offered me my first exciting glimpse into politics. I name my youngest son, "Curtis," in honor of Tulsa's first Black legislator. Twenty years later I would become an Oklahoma lawmaker.

The civil rights struggle was not without tragedy, with many leaders assassinated and many more civil rights workers killed. The war in Vietnam forced President Johnson to end his presidency. All the men whom I respected and were my political heroes were either dead or tarnished.

The 60's

Riots erupted in Watts, Chicago, Detroit, and more than 100 other cities. Thousands of antiwar protests converged on Chicago for the 1968 Democratic convention, and the resulting "police riot" was a watershed event of the 60s. In full glare of a national TV audience, they dramatically forced Americans to take sides on the war in Vietnam. The hippies influenced the direction of the Southeast Asian conflict and Richard Milhouse Nixon became the next president.

After bickering among its leaders, the Tulsa Chapter of Congress of Racial Equality disintegrated. The emergence of the Black power movement and the war had pushed most whites from the ranks of the Civil Rights Movement. The whites who remained involved in Tulsa were generally more radical than the Blacks. The assassinations left a vacuum in leadership and in purpose. Many of the former Tulsa militants became suit-wearing flunkies of the establishment, including myself, employed in LBJ's Great Society programs.

10
Black Wall Street Forgotten

Unqualified support for using the charred area for a railroad station.
                                        Tulsa Chamber of Commerce, 1921

TWO WHITE BOYS, Parrish Kelley and Larry Miller, are indelibly inked into my memory and responsible for returning me to activism. They reminded me of the *Readers Digest*'s "Most Unforgettable Characters I've Ever Met". The two hippies came to Tulsa as Volunteers in Service to America (VISTA). I credit them with reviving my interest in community organization, the Tulsa race riot, and politics.

One weekend the two shaggy-looking men appeared on my doorstep. Kelley's uncombed sandy hair was stacked over his ruddy, narrow face. The Harvard dropout's legs were two thirds of his lean body covered by jeans in bad need of mending, washing, or discarding. The VISTA volunteers were told they should talk to me about community organization. VISTA, a domestic Peace Corps, was a federal project designed to assist poor and working-class people in accessing their government and developing self-help projects.

Miller, an admitted socialist, was shorter, with a rounded choir boy baby face, square jaw and bright piercing eyes. He looked like Pee-wee Herman with an attitude. The patches on Miller's trousers had patches.

I was immediately put off when they said they had dropped out of college and signed on to VISTA to avoid military service in Vietnam. I asked: "So you're better-red-than-dead communists?"

Miller said, "Yes." For the next few minutes they conducted a seminar on the brewing conflict without convincing me the war was wrong. I was a committed bloodthirsty hawk.

Kelly said the VISTAs attended meetings of the Tulsa Park Board, examined records, and discovered the board was ordering playground equipment for parks in the Black community and then transferring it to the still-segregated parks for whites.

"I don't believe that," I said. "Lincoln Park is well-equipped." Lincoln was the historic park for Blacks.

"We're talking about Crawford Park."

"Crawford Park? I never heard of it."

Kelly opened a folder and showed me documents that showed a vacant, weeded area we called Yahola, was indeed officially named Crawford. Most of it was packed with trash. They wanted to use my name to convene a community meeting and make the information known.

"Look, white folks gonna do what white folks gonna do," I said. "I'm tired of fighting them. I got to go to work, and pushed the commie-inspired leftist out my door.

Three or four days later they were on my porch again. The two asked me to help them design a handbill calling for a meeting to expose the thievery of the park equipment. "That's all," they said.

I relented and drew up a handbill titled "You are Negroes, not Tulsans." Being "Negro" was out of fashion. We were only comfortable with being Black. The handbill had pictures of the weedy, trash-filled, and unknown Crawford Park. It carried a list of park equipment—the swings, seesaws, slides, carousels, picnic tables and the rest—that had been ordered and never delivered, but instead transferred to white parks. I signed the handbill and called for a Saturday gathering in an auditorium of a nearby Catholic school controlled by an activist priest.

Kelly took the handbill to a printer who immediately leaked it to the press. The next day the handbill story was all over the media. Editorials accused the VISTA workers of attempting to incite trouble among the races. In short order, Congressman Page Belcher called for a federal investigation of the VISTA program.

When contacted by the press, I told the reporter I had written the handbill. They ignored my confession, blaming the VISTAs and focused on Belcher's assault on the federal program. The controversy gained a kind of attention we never could have gained just passing out the handbills in front of supermarkets. What is more, most of the old-guard Black leaders, including the influential Rev. Ben H. Hill, were also unaware of Crawford Park. The preacher and the old guard agreed with the handbill's assertion.

"I've been saying this for years (you are Negroes, not Tulsans)," Rev. Hill said to the press and announced his endorsement of the meeting. "I will be there." Two years later Rev. Hill was elected to the Oklahoma legislature.

On Saturday morning, the auditorium was packed, standing room only. Even the old guard was present. The rally drew white Catholics, Unitarians, and restless liberals. Kelly masterfully presented a convincing slideshow. Black leaders called for new equipment for north side parks, a Black park board member and a commitment that the decimation would never happen again. Caught up in the emotion, I called for a march on City Hall. There was thunderous applause.

A new organization, Citizens for Progress (CFP), was formed to initiate action needed to press our demands. I remember Betty Fricke fondly as CFP's most dedicated soul. The white woman quit her job to work full time for the organization. The meeting also pulled in Black professionals who had remained on the sidelines during the civil rights demonstrations.

Dr. Charles Lewis, a dentist, became CFP's chairman and Dr. Charles Christopher was named secretary. The mayor requested a meeting and quickly all of CFP's demands were met. The well-liked Booker T. Washington High School coach, Ed Lacy, became the first Black member of the park board. Tennis courts and new equipment were added. When I complained that "we don't play tennis yet," a basketball court was added at Lincoln Park. Some years later, Lincoln Park was renamed to honor the popular football coach.

During the negotiations, I may have become the conscience of Mrs. P.P. Manion, a rich matriarch who served as the park board's chairperson. In a weak moment, during a public meeting, she triggered laughter when she called me her "Negro" son. I denied the illegitimate relationship, but we became great friends.

After the park board confrontations, I retreated back into my pursuit of the American Dream. Again, my race to the middle class was interrupted by Kelley and Miller. The VISTA's attention had turned to racial justice in relation to economic development and historical truth-telling. They came to me with a notion that changed my life and would come into fruition nearly 30 years later.

They said Tulsa needs to remember what happened in 1921. They said that the buildings and shacks on Greenwood Avenue were historic and demonstrate North Tulsa's resilience to racist attacks. Greenwood should be dedicated as an historic area to be acknowledged, visited, and maintained.

According to them, Greenwood was the largest civilian killing field in American history. "Only the Civil War was worse."

I knew this. Yet they complained that there was not one plaque, marker, or any mention that a riot happened. I had never noticed that. They suggested if churches became involved perhaps a museum or memorial could mark the event.

"It could draw visitors to the area to learn this vital history, pay homage to the community's resilience and even help revive the dying business sector on Greenwood," Miller explained.

They reminded me of my youthful conversation with my high school teachers. I was 15 years old at the time and called my teacher a liar when he said Greenwood Avenue had been burned to the ground and over 300 people killed.

The riot and its aftermath had remained a part of my consciousness, even though I had no idea what to do about it. A museum sounded like a good idea that even white people might support. We needed to get the Black preachers involved.

I was the Labor Affairs Director of the Tulsa Urban League, one of President Johnson's Great Society programs designed to recruit Blacks into the apprenticeship programs of the building and construction trades. After becoming the first Black unionized baker at the Wonder Bread Company in Tulsa, and the first Black records clerk at American Airlines, I was truly a child of LBJ's affirmative action.

My employment at the Urban League had shocked nearly everyone, including myself. During the Civil Rights Movement, the league's director, Marion Taylor, had called us troublemakers and suggested that segregation and discrimination disputes could be settled over a cup of coffee. After 300 years of drinking coffee, Taylor's idea came down to many, many lynched souls drenched in caffeine.

Even though the League had recruited me for "two good jobs," I crashed a board meeting and demanded and received Taylor's resignation. The board refused to accept his quitting. A year or so later, Taylor repeatedly called my house leaving urgent messages for me to come to his office. I wasn't about to consort with that Uncle Tom and refused to return the calls. The Rev. T. Oscar Chappelle, a League board member, reached me and explained what Taylor had in mind was a job for me. I met the League director and I was hired and we became great friends. His only direction was: "Make something happen. These union boys are tough bigots."

Much later, I discussed the VISTA idea with Taylor. His impression was that Blacks wanted to forget the riot and whites might react with hostility to any discussions of it. He said white folks were afraid of crossing Archer St., Tulsa's Mason-Dixon line. Taylor suggested I talk with Rev. Chappelle. "Chappelle controls those preachers," he declared.

The Baptist minister listened intently as the two VISTA volunteers unveiled their idea for a memorial. He set a meeting with Black leaders and preachers. Even though the three of us arrived to the meeting early, already sitting in the large sanctuary with Rev. Chappelle were NAACP leader and attorney Amos Hall and Ed Goodwin, Sr., publisher of the weekly Black newspaper, the *Oklahoma Eagle*. They were arguably the most influential leaders in the Black community.

The Rev. Chappelle was not only the controlling boss of the local Baptist ministers, he was president of the state organization, and also held the third highest rank in the National Baptist Convention. As the pastor of one of Tulsa's largest churches, Rev. Chappelle would later serve as my campaign treasurer when I was elected to the Oklahoma legislature. He recruited preachers and raised much of the money for my election.

Hall was the titular head of the local and state NAACP and head of the National Conference of Grand Masters Prince Hall Masons, and as such he was in charge of Black Shriners throughout the world. The lawyer was good friends with the future Supreme Court Justice Thurgood Marshall and had served as Marshall's lead attorney on the groundbreaking *Sipuel v. Board of Regents of the University of Oklahoma* Supreme Court decision. The plaintiff, Ada Louise Sipuel, was raised in Chickasha, where her father moved after his church was burned to the ground in 1921. She was the first Black student to enter the University of Oklahoma law school after this landmark decision outlawed segregation in higher education. Later, Hall became Oklahoma's first Black judge.

Goodwin, a wealthy member of a pioneering family, was a riot refugee and had been held in a concentration camp during the 1921 race riot. He was also a law school classmate and friend of the current governor. He had named his third son after Robert Kerr, another friend, who was a close ally of LBJ. All three men became my mentors, counselors, and formidable heroes in my life. Even today I can hear their voices cheering or chastising me about something I did well or badly.

When I think of these men, I remember them as smart, down-to-earth, respected, formal, and sophisticated. They were comfortable with poor and working people. They could wear a white tuxedo with high-top brown steel-toe boots and not be considered out of fashion but trendsetters. Still, they were afraid of yesterday. I suspect they believed our freedom would come sooner or later, as long as I didn't make white folks too mad during the wait. Until then, they languished in angry anticipation.

After a bit of meaningless chatter, the preacher opened the meeting. "I guess nobody else is coming."

I explained the idea of a riot memorial. Mount Zion, Paradise, Vernon, Christ Temple, and several other Black churches were destroyed in 1921 and I was hopeful Black churches might take the lead in the project. Growing up I had been a member of all the churches, easily recruited from the one to another by the refreshments offered.

The Rev. Chappelle told us that after the riot his father, P.A. Chappelle, joined B.C. Franklin and I.H. Spears to practice law from a tent and won a lawsuit against the city that found the post-riot fire ordinance unconstitutional. He said that Greenwood's continued existence is the direct result of the efforts of his father and these lawyers. The Baptist minister said most of the preachers of today moved to Tulsa long after the riot and had little passion for this history. "Their absence today is testimony to that indifference."

"There is good progress," Hall reminded the three of us. "Schools are being integrated. There are Blacks working at the Douglas bomber plant and American Airlines. A downtown store had a Black elevator operator not so far from where the riot was triggered." Pointing at me he said, "Don, you were the first Black baker in the state, had other good jobs and now you're helping young people earn a good living in labor unions. White repentance has come slow, but it is moving." There was no response when I noted they had to be pushed during the Civil Rights Movement.

Pointing to the two VISTA workers, Goodwin was more direct, "After these white boys stir up trouble, they're going to move on to other causes and vanish. Then we'll be stuck with dealing with these crazy white folks, some of whom had a hand in burning down our side of town." He said his dad, J.H. Goodwin, had lost more than $50,000 in the riot and had made the first and largest contribution to build Mount Zion Baptist Church. The $85,000 church was destroyed 30 days after its completion.

"Black Wall Street is a myth," Goodwin noted. "Businesses were piled on Greenwood because Blacks were not allowed to spend money in white establishments. For every café, there were three juke joints and gambling dens. There were more pimps, prostitutes, hoodlums, and numbers runners than doctors, lawyers and teachers. Then and now it only attracts ambulances and outlaws at night."

These elders suffered from the lingering fear related to the riot, racism, and the economic fallout from desegregation. "They want our money but they don't want us," the publisher explained.

As the meeting closed the Rev. Chappelle said he would talk with and call another meeting with the other preachers. He never did. The issue was closed. Years later he confessed to me that he had only contacted Hall and Goodwin about that meeting with the VISTAs.

Few of us active in the Civil Rights Movement anticipated that desegregation would invite the decline of the historic Greenwood area. In the late 1960s, with the rigid segregation eased more and more, pent-up dollars began to flow outside the Black business district's borders.

In its heyday during the 40s and 50s, Greenwood Avenue and its surrounding neighborhoods could boast of as many as 500 businesses and professional offices. As the 1970s approached there were five, and urban renewal bulldozers were poised on the boundaries of the Black ghetto to demolish the brick carcasses. The Dreamland Theater, the most noteworthy symbol of resilience, was among the first buildings crumpled by the bulldozer. Goodwin later purchased urban renewal options and the remnants of the famed avenue, leading to its redevelopment.

What generally goes unnoticed is that Black Wall Street is only a mile long. Tulsa streets are named alphabetically. There is no Greenwood Avenue, or for that matter a "G" street that extends south into the white community.

To the north, Greenwood dead-ends at the white community border and is renamed Garrison, a fitting and proper name for whites who garrisoned themselves in the racist enclave and feared any contact with the Black neighbors who surrounded them. Tulsa's famous Gap Band draws its name from the Black community's basic borders—"Greenwood, Archer and Pine."

In 1958, Johnny Gamble, an African-American entrepreneur, penetrated the white garrison separating the races. His house was bombed. Before the Gamble bombing there were cross burnings. Within a stone's throw of the encroaching Black community, the White Citizen Council had held open meetings at John Burroughs Elementary School and the Cincinnati Avenue Christian Church.

Bigoted white neighbors advertised their displeasure on billboards and with leaflets. Nonetheless, integration into the separated area stirred white flight. In time, at any intersection in the ghetto, a jaywalker could be run down by the parade of moving vans.

I remained involved with Kelley, Miller, and other VISTAs orchestrating confrontations with "the establishment." CFP picketed aerospace and other companies demanding equal employment and an end to housing discrimination. When the school board attempted to close the all-Black historic Carver Junior High, CFP, the Urban League, and NAACP were involved in creating "freedom schools" and held the children out for several months until the board relented. I was a founder of CFP, served on the NAACP board and was a League staff member. The war with the school board over closing Carver was chiefly responsible for creating magnet schools in the city. This brought white students to the inner city and the appointment and later election of the city's first Black school board member. Carver is now considered one of the best middle schools in the nation.

While CORE was picketing segregated business in the early 60s, Goodwin's son Ed Jr., asked me to report on CORE activities for the *Oklahoma Eagle*. A weekly column, *Lines from the Ghetto*, emerged from that reporting. The column was a no-holds-barred satirical assault on the Tulsa white business establishment, Uncle Toms, and political bosses. The essays catapulted me into becoming the city's leading and only Black muckraker. I was called on to write columns for the white newspapers, and my picture appeared on the cover of the Chamber of Commerce Magazine, and in history books describing Black anger.

My involvement was not without a downside. I was the senior staff member of the Urban League. When the Director's job became open, I applied and was turned down. The reason given was the job required a master's degree.

However, the former director, with the same educational deficiency as me, had been allowed a provisional certification and hired. Al Mankoff, a board member and friend, told me privately that my outspokenness in the press and my militant CFP activities had disqualified me for the job as a leader of the more moderate organization.

At the time, there was a push to place more Blacks in the media after the Kerner Report made such recommendations. The report, co-chaired by former Oklahoma U.S. Senator Fred Harris, examined the roots of the nationwide riots in the late 1960s and pressed for programs and affirmative action to correct racial imbalances.

Mankoff, who had told me the real reason for my rejection by the Urban League, was a fan of my weekly column.

He was now the director of human resources for Peat, Marwick, Mitchell and Company. Their executive search was intended to find an editor for the *Post-Tribune* in Gary, Indiana. He recommended me, and an interview in Chicago with *Post-Tribune* executives went well. Then, almost as an afterthought, I was asked the major qualifying question: "Can you type?"

In the ninth grade, I had been lured into a typing class following the same tall beauty who led me into discovering the riot in high school. However, the typing teacher allowed no talking and I was forced to learn the one finger method. When I was asked about my typing skills, I recalled my first love. I had not touched a typewriter for more than 20 years and had just barely passed the class.

I answered, "You betcha."

Clockwise from top left:
Young Pearline Vann "Mama", Isaac Evitt, Uncle Do-Baby

James Evitt with his wife Liza Jones (left) and Mary "Big Mama" Jones Evitt

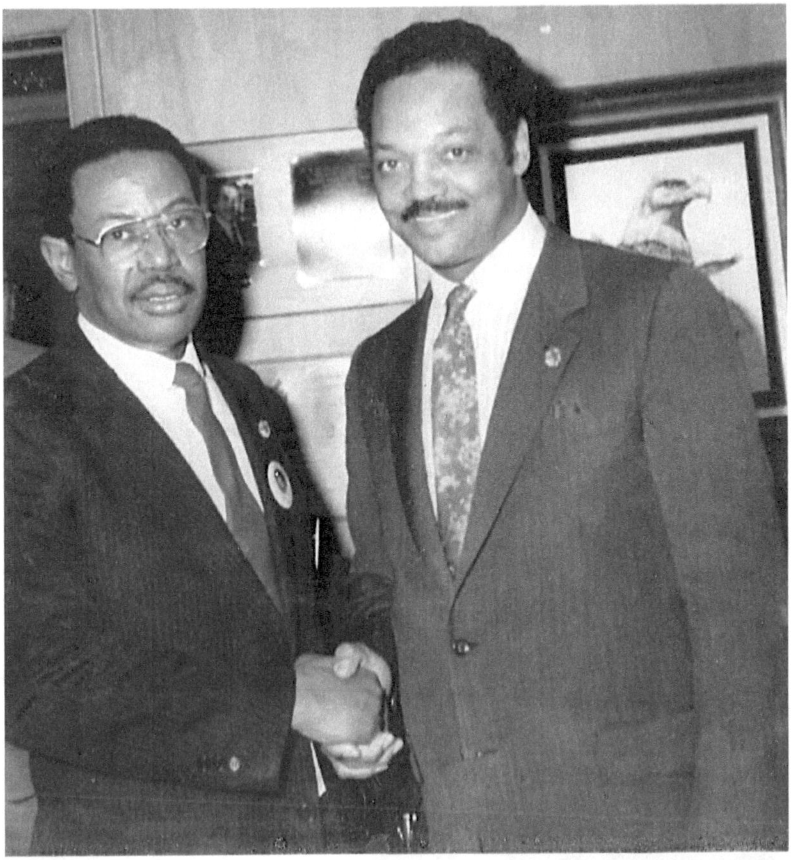

Top: Rep. Don Ross with Rev. Jesse Jackson

Right: Front Page of *The Oklahoma Eagle* announcing Rep. Ross winning the District 73 Primary, his initial bid for the Oklahoma House Seat

Miss Black Tulsa Ebony Fashion Fair model

Mitchell's ballet to be performed during Diamond Jubilee

Greenwood goes to the movies

The Oklahoma Eagle

The Black Voice of Northeast Oklahoma

McIntyre, Ross capture primary votes

Hide and seek results in slaying

Man in jail for mother's gun

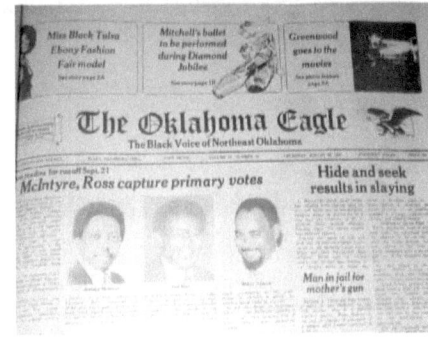

Top: Rep. Ross on the house floor giving an impassioned speech about the Confederate flag flying above the Oklahoma State Capitol

Top facing: Donna Ross (daughter), former Miss America and R&B vocalist Vanessa Williams, Rep. Ross

Bottom facing: Rep. Ross with Olympic Gold Medalist Kenny Monday and a member of the Oklahoma State House of Representatives

Top: Rep. Ross with Ed Dwight, Jr. unveiling a photograph of post-destruction Greenwood

Bottom: Rep. Ross featured in *Tulsa People* Magazine

Top facing: Children of Don and Diane Ross. From left to right: Ronald Ross, Reginald Ross, Edward Ross, Kavin Ross, Donna Ross (seated) **Bottom:** Rep. Ross pictured with some of many grandchildren on their Mid-Atlantic History Tour

Top: The plaque displayed outside of the Greenwood Cultural Center noting the destruction of the Zulu Lounge.

Bottom: Rep. Ross with the family elders and his siblings. From left to right: Floyd Vann Jr., Mildred Evitt, Lonzo Ross, Ethel Vann, Floyd Vann Sr. Pearlie Ross, Don Ross, Ben Ricketts, James Ross. Photo is from Pearline Vann's homegoing.

11
A Black Quota

It is not just the Negroes, but it is all of us, who must overcome the crippling legacy of bigotry and injustice. And we shall overcome.
                                        President Lyndon B. Johnson

I BECAME THE ASSISTANT to the Managing Editor of the *Post-Tribune* in Gary, Indiana. Darrow "Duke" Tully told me I was only the nation's second Black in an executive position with a metropolitan daily newspaper.

Tully apologized for the deteriorating condition of the Steel City. I had arrived a day earlier. A classmate living in Chicago had taken me on a tour of Gary. The most depressing part of the visit was seeing, in the shadow of City Hall, a ten-story or more Goodwill Industries building in the heart of what was left of downtown. The building had been donated to the agency to avoid paying taxes on it as whites fled the majority-Black city.

I told him it looked like my neighborhood in Tulsa, nothing new, nothing scary. "I like its Blackness," I said. I think the answer pleased him. At the time I didn't realize Gary was an urban Vietnam, with drug gangs at war over turf and blue-collar white ethnic groups battling to maintain some feeling of entitlement.

Steel City also produced The Jackson Five and I was a fan of the band. The modest four-room, one-bathroom home of the Jacksons offered few clues of how 11 family members navigated through their daily routine.

In 1968, the Northwest Indiana city had been pushed into national attention when it elected Richard Gordon Hatcher as the nation's first Black mayor. As more and more Blacks were drawn from the South to the steel mills, whites fled to the outlying counties. After

Hatcher's election, all but a few hearty souls, mostly European ethnic and Jewish, joined the exodus.

Merrillville, a sleepy little bedroom community of white Gary expatriates, exploded in population and restrictive housing codes enforced its segregation. Whites wanted no link to Blacks or Gary. East Gary, a small-town next door, changed its name to Lake Station to correct any mistaken identification with the crime-ridden city politically controlled by Blacks.

Gary lacked any economic anticipation. Greenwood was destroyed by riot, but Gary was pillaged from abandonment. The city's only hotel closed shortly after I arrived. Drug-related killings were everyday occurrences. The police were known more for their corruption than for any commitment to protect and serve. The *Post-Tribune* was a white island surrounded by a sea of nearly 70 percent Black population.

The newspaper made a practice of placing the ghastly photographs of the latest victim of gang warfare on its front page, offending the city's Black middle class and further emptying the city of whites. With the exception of a lady working on the Women's Page and a photographer, Blacks worked only in the newspaper circulation department.

Practicing typing hours upon hours, I soon acquired the skill only to learn I was hired to be seen as the spook near the door. The only qualification I needed was to be Black and breathing. From my key vantage point I showcased my Blackness month after month with little else to do. Doing nothing is hard work, particularly when white colleagues were giggling while quietly confirming their certainty of my incompetence.

I did land one scoop. Julian "Cannonball" Adderley was performing a weeklong engagement in Gary. I had hung out with the jazz saxophonist and his brother, Nat, for much of that week, when tragedy struck. Cannonball suffered a stroke and was sent to Gary's St. Mary Mercy hospital. While reading the early edition of the paper, I saw that he was merely listed as "hospitalized" and nothing else. The reporter had no idea who the jazz innovator was.

I alerted the city desk and pulled together an extensive story discussing his condition and his place in the jazz world. The story and picture were bumped to the front page in the later edition and sent to the Associated Press. My daily dispatches on his condition were printed all over the world. After Cannonball died, four weeks following the stroke, my brief entrée into the world of journalism passed with him and I returned to a lonely station near the door. I was miserable.

There was one good side. I had an unlimited expense account to entertain. Without it, I would have never learned about the three-martini lunch. Friends often traveled through nearby Chicago and I took them dining at the best places. One time I met Tulsans Dr. Lawrence Reed and his wife, Jayne, who were attending a medical convention in the Windy City.

They were housed at the exclusive Ambassador West Hotel. I offered to take them to the hotel's fabulous "Pump Room" for dinner. It was a fun evening until the waiter came. I ordered steak tartare. I thought it was something exotic like a T-Bone steak cooked in tartar sauce. We returned to our chatter.

After a while the waiter returned and served my friends lobsters and left. Moments later he returned with a big metal bowl and was mixing stuff in it. I assumed he was preparing the Caesar salad until he placed the dish before me.

"What is this?"

"Sir, you did order steak tartare, didn't you?"

"Yes, but this ain't no T-Bone."

"Sir, steak tartare is marinated ground beef."

"Raw?"

"Yes, sir."

"Well you just take that back to the kitchen and put some fire under it," I demanded. I can now boast of eating the most expensive meat loaf in Chicago, maybe in the entire world.

On another occasion, the National Urban League was hosting a conference in Chicago. I invited about ten former colleagues to Arthur's, the legendary jazz club. Ramsey Lewis was the featured entertainer.

I wanted so much to impress them with my new status and told them "get what you want." I ordered several bottles of the best wine, even sent wine to a couple who were just married. We closed out dinner with the restaurant's most expensive liqueur.

Among all my expense account foibles, it was the record tab. I spread several credit cards on the table and arrogantly told the waiter, "Close your eyes and pull one."

She answered: "Sir, you didn't notice the sign on the table. Arthur's is closing for good tonight and it's cash only!"

My wife and kids were completely oblivious of my misery at the *Post-Tribune*. Our house was near Lake Michigan. During the summer, Diane walked our six small children to the beach and they whiled away the lazy days on the polluted banks of Lake Michigan.

I spent nearly five years exhibiting a phenomenal skill of sitting without complaint and doing nothing. Then I began whining to my bosses and was allowed a weekly column. I satirized politicians, gang members, cops, recalcitrant whites, shallow Blacks, and other haughty notables. The column gained much popularity.

My friend Geoffrey Brown, *Jet* magazine Managing Editor, had a Washington, D.C., office that was housed on the same floor with *Washington Post* syndicated columnist Art Buchwald. Brown passed on some of my columns to the humorist. (Geoffrey was killed in a car accident, shortly after he married actress-singer Diahann Carroll.)

Buchwald became a good friend. He founded the fictional National Association of Humor Writers that included Erma Bombeck, Russell Baker, Jerry Nachman, Art Hoppe, and Robert Yoakum. Buchwald invited me into the group and joked, I think, that I was invited "as a quota" for their affirmative action program. I still have reams of hilarious letters from all the writers. Buchwald promoted the group in *Time* magazine and he called me a talented humor columnist. We talked of developing our letters into a book, but nothing came of it.

I last visited Buchwald in Edgartown, his summer home on Martha's Vineyard, and attended what would be his last celebrity charity auction. I sat among television personalities Walter Cronkite, Mike Wallace, and Diane Sawyer, movie star Patricia Neal, country singer Linda Ronstadt, historian David McCullough, cartoonist Jules Feiffer, and other rich and famous celebrities who made the island hideaway their summer home.

Later that year the cigar-smoking humorist taped his last interview, to be broadcast after his death: "I'm Art Buchwald and I'm dead." As he did in life, Buchwald had the last laugh even in death.

Writing a weekly column didn't soak up much of my time. Finally, with lethargic bravery, I sucked up to the publisher and asked to lead a team of reporters focusing on racial issues in the county. He reluctantly approved the project.

After spending several weeks writing a series on housing segregation and other racial complexities throughout the area, word of the project leaked out to the white establishment. The publisher mulled over whether to print the stories or not. He finally relented and the series won a statewide Associated Press award. The paper gave the award little notice in its publication. By then, I had made up my mind to leave.

My friend Ernest Green, the famed first graduate of Central High School in Little Rock, Arkansas, had been named by President Carter as an Assistant Secretary of Labor. Green offered me the job as his deputy assistant. The job required a good deal of travel.

My wife and I found a house we could afford in a distant all-white Virginia suburb. Diane was extremely shy and didn't meet people easily. I had some concerns about the cultural shock of moving her and the family from nearly all-Black Gary to a virtually all-white Washington, D.C., suburb. Until then, I would wager she never had as much as a 10-minute conversation with anybody white. Meanwhile, I was offered another job back home. Instead of moving to Washington, D.C., I returned to Tulsa as Vice-President and General Manager of the *Oklahoma Eagle*.

Another reason for my leaving Gary was that the *Post-Tribune*'s emphasis was changing. As reporters and editors were moving into the suburbs that surrounded the Black community, the impact, economics and pain of the migration was ignored. Banks, department stores, hotels, and other industries left the city. The *Post-Tribune* became more of a booster for the exodus than a voice attempting to at least explain the white flight. What was bad for Gary was good for the suburbs and its allies at the newspaper.

Gary had its problems. Drugs, crime, street gangs, nearly daily murders, and the city's major employer, U.S. Steel, was planning on shutting down. Even the Chamber of Commerce packed up and left.

While Diane supported the move to Washington, I could tell she preferred moving back to Tulsa and being closer to her aging mother in New Mexico. The kids wanted to remain in Gary.

Kavin, the oldest, had become fairly proficient at playing the bass guitar and had taught his brother Edward the instrument. Reggie and Ronnie had shown skills as basketball players. Curtis's teacher called him the smartest kid in the class. Donna enjoyed her role as the baby and was spoiled by all of us. The greatest complaint from the boys was leaving the school, their friends, and the beach.

The *Post-Tribune* offered me another fancy title and a pay increase to remain. However, the deciding factor for Diane and me came when our son Reggie reported to us that in the grade school bathroom, he was offered a puff from a marijuana cigarette.

The drug culture had taken hold in the all-Black sections of Gary and was now creeping into our comfortable neighborhood. I turned down the $10,000 raise from the *Post-Tribune* and headed home to Tulsa at a $5,000 cut in my annual salary. I have never regretted the $15,000 annual income swing. Gary was a five-year adventure and while there, by osmosis, I had become a journalist. Reflecting back, I gained some life-long friends and, with some help, learned much about myself, Black leadership, and the challenges of relationships between African-American and white people: Whites could escape the complicated sociology, while Blacks were either a part of the malaise or trapped in it.

On moving to Gary, Green had placed me in contact with his friend, a Little Rock native named Jackie Shropshire. In turn, Jackie introduced me to his former law partner, Richard G. Hatcher, the nation's first Black mayor of a major American city, and many other movers and shakers of the Steel City.

In time I crept toward credibility among my colleagues and I became close friends to key members of Hatcher's administration. When there were disagreements with the mayor, or between the many City Hall factions, one side or the other leaked the deal to me

A Black Quota

and the story found itself in the pages of the *Post-Tribune*. On many occasions the mayor first heard of his feuding departments in the newspaper.

One of the really big secrets exposed was when the bachelor mayor was to elope. It was so secret, only about five people outside the family knew. I was told and promptly announced the wedding plans in the paper and to the nation.

The *Post-Tribune* news people were friendly enough, and perhaps even leaning toward being social liberals, but it appeared to me that I was still not one of them and could never be. For them, my job was not to be a newsman, but to satisfy a quota and serve as eyes into the Black community. There wasn't anything I could do to change that.

Watching my friends in City Hall pushing and shoving and exercising influence taught me politics was the new Civil Rights Movement and was essential in getting things accomplished for Black people. Mayor Hatcher had attracted first-rate Black professionals from all over the country. This talent was not only drawn to City Hall, but the banks and corporations recruited them also.

Blacks owned the local cable TV franchise, managed millions of dollars in federal and local programs, and yes, a Black newspaper executive was recruited for Gary's only daily newspaper. Blacks controlled the airport authority and other major boards and commissions. In Gary whites were recruited for affirmative action.

Before moving to Gary, I viewed electoral politics in the simplest of terms: Rarely, if ever, did I vote for a Republican; white Democrats were the lesser of the evils and Tulsa's lone Black elected official in the Oklahoma legislature was there to press civil rights issues.

On leaving Gary, I was poised to question why Tulsa Blacks were only employed at the street department lifting garbage and as janitors at City Hall. Blacks were appointed to the school and park boards only after protest. Why weren't Blacks eligible to serve on other boards and commissions? Why couldn't Tulsa businesses recruit engineers, bankers, lawyers, architects and other Black professionals, as I had seen in Gary?

Incidentally, Darrow "Duke" Tully, who hired me in Gary, became publisher of the *Arizona Republic* and the *Phoenix Gazette*. Tully is credited for jumpstarting U.S. Senator John McCain's political career. I had listened to Tully's adventures as a pilot in Korea and Vietnam. They were powerful and mesmerizing tales. They were also untrue. Tully had never been in the military and was shamed out of the Arizona power establishment.

After returning home, I spent a year with the *Oklahoma Eagle*, then resigned and, in 1978, established Ebony Partners, a public relations and executive search firm. I proceeded with some success as a consultant to some of the city's largest firms in challenging the glass ceilings limiting professional opportunities for Blacks in Tulsa. I had learned in Gary that politics not only encompassed civil rights, it enshrined and protected them.

In 1982, I sought and won a seat in the Oklahoma legislature. Entering the race was a fluke. Penny Williams was a wealthy white liberal and former Republican. She was involved in the Urban League, school integration, and other community-based organizations to which I also belonged. Now a Democrat, she was seeking a heavily GOP seat in the Oklahoma House of Representatives.

Penny was the former wife of Joseph Williams, board chairman of Oklahoma's largest corporation. Joseph Williams, also my friend, had awarded my firm its first contract to recruit Black executives for The Williams Companies. The contract launched my PR firm and opened the door to recruit Blacks for other large companies.

I asked Dr. Lawrence Reed, Oklahoma's leading Black surgeon and his wife, Jayne, to host a fundraising event in their palatial home for Penny. In 1978, the nearly $1,500 raised was the largest political fundraiser held in the African-American community. Williams later credited the events as financially launching her more than 25 years of a very successful career in the Oklahoma House and Senate.

It hadn't occurred to me to challenge Bernard J. McIntyre, the popular incumbent in the Oklahoma House of Representatives. There were loud whispers about McIntyre's drug use and his failure to push for Black interests. We were friends and raised four doors apart in a housing project. Rumors aside, I personally liked McIntyre and had worked hard for his first election. One afternoon, I was headed back to my downtown office and he cut me off in his two-seater Mercedes convertible.

There was much talk on how he could afford such a car while earning less than $10,000 a year. He faced reelection in just a few weeks. As usual, he had drawn only token opposition and was heading toward an easy victory.

McIntyre learned of the fundraiser for Williams and told me he was going down to a certain defeat in his race if I didn't help him raise the money for a critical last mailing. He needed $1,000. I became angry and asked, "Why would you hustle me? You will win with 80 to 90 percent of the vote? Furthermore, you haven't done one damn thing for our community since you've been in office. I'm going to run against your butt the next time." I said it without thinking. "You will likely win, but I promise this time you will know you've been in a race."

He cursed and sped off.

McIntyre won reelection handily, as I had predicted. The next day I began my race to unseat him. I was surprised, even shocked, at people who offered their support for my candidacy. The Reverend T. Oscar Chappelle, the most influential minister in Oklahoma, volunteered to become my campaign treasurer.

Thelma Whitlow, the well-known wife of my high school principal, H.C. Whitlow, signed on as the campaign manager. She brought with her most of my teachers, many of whom had either flunked or nearly flunked me at Booker T. Washington High School. Mr. Whitlow, who had once told me "I don't know what you could be," wrote my largest check, for $200.

Meanwhile, campaigning left little time for home life. Thingamajigs around the house went unrepaired. Much to Diane's consternation, when I was home I relieved the children from her stern discipline and took them to the amusement park, for ice cream or to the movies. Daddy was the darling of the kids.

I remember the very day she decided enough was enough. There was a leaky pipe under the sink. She ordered me to fix it. I told her to call a plumber. She raised so much hell I acquiesced, went to Sears and bought every possible wrench I might need. I crawled under the sink. The wrench slipped off the pipe and I skinned my knuckles. I packed up the tools, took them back to Sears, and called a plumber. He fixed the leak in less than five minutes and presented a bill for $50.

The anger that framed her face was the first hint that I had traded the plumber's five minutes for 22 years of marriage. She never complained after that, even though the campaign and other activities soaked up more and more of my time.

In my campaign, Mrs. Whitlow and Reverend Chappelle gathered the endorsements of most of the prominent members of our community. However, we couldn't even come close to penetrating McIntyre's strength: the working class and union vote.

Then, one late evening, State Rep. Penny Williams called me. A Democrat, she had won the strongly Republican district easily. The Oklahoma legislature was in the process of reapportionment through which a majority Black senate seat was created. McIntyre sought election to it. I gained the union support and won election to the House seat and McIntyre won in the Senate. However, the new senator was caught using drugs in a sting operation. In 1986, McIntyre was indicted for cocaine use and sent to prison. I was the campaign manager for Maxine Horner, a good friend and political ally, in her race for McIntyre's unexpired term. She won and became the first Black female elected to the Oklahoma Senate.

Meanwhile, Diane had calmly asked me to leave and filed for divorce in the middle of the primary campaign. It was an amicable departure. We shared the same lawyer, drove to court together and had dinner the evening after a judge approved the separation. As a parting gift I gave her a ring with her birthstone and she gave me a set of crescent wrenches. We both laughed. Six children, twelve grandchildren, and three great-grandchildren later, we continue to share a very close relationship.

During my time in the legislature, Tim McVeigh's 1995 bombing of Oklahoma City's Alfred P. Murrah Federal Building would become a disturbing reminder of the bombing of Black Wall Street more than 75 years before.

The Oklahoma City bombing was called the nation's worst act of terrorism.

Not so.
I would have an opportunity to make my case.

12
Riot Scars

Things bygone are the only things that last.
                                        Eugene Lee Hamilton

THE GREENWOOD CULTURAL CENTER was a vision of Black Wall Street pioneer Katie C. Duckery, and two members of the Volunteers in Service to America. That vision had been Mrs. Duckery's passion for more than 25 years. I sought public office for the most part to bring her dream into fruition.

The idea of the center was obsessively etched into my consciousness during a mass meeting of Greenwood-area citizens with Tulsa's mayor and other city officials. A riot survivor, Mrs. Duckery spoke for many of the older residents when she tearfully reminded the crowded room of 500 or more people that Black Wall Street had a rich and proud history; how the area and its people had survived a brutal riot and lost everything.

"Yet we brought Greenwood back," she cried, "bigger and better than before." She said the riot was caused because evil white people wanted the Black-owned land, "And that's why there are bulldozers at our gate now—they still want the land!"

Urban renewal was set to knock down the old buildings from bygone days. To the roar of applause, Mrs. Duckery recalled achievements where so many fortunes of a dejected people matured and prospered. "There must be something left to their memory and for the generations of children who will live under the shadow they cast and the scars left from the riot."

I was captured by Mrs. Duckery's emotional plea. The VISTA volunteers had proposed a similar idea years before. It had been rejected by the elders out of fear of antagonizing white people. Her stirring reminder had reconnected me to the idea. As with Gettysburg, Normandy, The Little Big Horn and other battlegrounds, these hallowed 35 square blocks of deteriorating buildings had to be preserved to honor the riot survivors and their resilience.

More than two decades later the $3.5 million Greenwood Cultural Center became the commemoration Mrs. Duckery envisioned, remembering the African-American boulevard's battered history and dogged elasticity. Restricted by segregation and discrimination, Greenwood's pioneers and their unbroken spirit would be remembered through pictorial exhibits of Black Wall Street, the 1921 massacre and the district's resurgence.

The cultural center opened in 1996 and has proudly carried out the mission to preserve Tulsa's African-American heritage. The center is important testimony to the idea that we can never forget the past. The vision is also to promote positive images of the African-American community by providing educational, art and cultural experiences with an array of offerings for youth interaction and involvement.

The Greenwood Cultural Center would never have gotten off the ground had it not been for the very rightwing mayor, now U.S. Senator James Inhofe. When I approached Mayor Inhofe about the idea, he didn't blink or require a study; he offered $25,000 in city development funds for the planning, and donated $500 personally.

Even though I've made hundreds of speeches as a "yellow dog" Democrat against him and other rightwing Republicans, they were the elected officials who positively impacted my community.

In addition to the Greenwood Cultural Center, Inhofe supported the development and funding of the multi-million-dollar Westview Medical Clinic. It was to be owned and operated by Blacks. He also named the first and the only Black to fill a vacancy at the City Commission, and then the Black commissioner was elected citywide. My appreciation for Inhofe was a bit conflicting.

I actively campaigned against him when a friend and progressive Democrat Terry Young sought the mayor's office. At a strategy session of ten or so Young supporters, they were all but ready to surrender to the inevitability of Inhofe's reelection. As the meeting was breaking up without even a plan for a second meeting, I announced: "Inhofe has said he doesn't need the Black vote to win." The room was now filled with anger and energy and eager anticipation of firing the mayor.

There was not so one small problem.

I had lied.

Inhofe never said that.

At the barbershop several days later, I was asked if I had heard that Mayor Inhofe had said he didn't need the Black vote. "We'll show him!" came the mumbles in angry solidarity. Even more, in the beauty shops, Black churches, bars, young and old, everyone united for throwing Inhofe out. A rightwing Republican had united the Black community for the first and only time. Even during the Civil Rights Movement, Black unity was a toss-up. Most preachers ducked the movement, but preached against Inhofe from their pulpits.

There was a record turnout among Blacks. Young was unexpectedly elected mayor, winning by less than 500 votes. He collected all but a very few votes in the Black precincts. The tale has dogged Inhofe in every election since.

I've only confessed the Inhofe lie to former Oklahoma Governor David Walters. In 2002, Walters was running against Inhofe for the U.S. Senate. He wanted to press the Inhofe tale in the campaign. I told him I started that lie. I should tell the U.S. Senator that I'm sorry, but it just ain't in me. Matter of fact he owes me. Had it not been for me, he would have never left city government to be elected to the House and later the Senate. I do owe the American people an apology for inflicting Inhofe on them.

I openly supported Republican mayors James Hewgley and Robert LaFortune and have never regretted it. After Hewgley won his election in a landslide, despite his pouring millions of dollars into the Black community, he only received a tiny fraction of their votes.

He asked me what happened. Dr. Martin Luther King, Jr., had been assassinated and riots had erupted in several cities. I told the mayor all the militants voted for him. He wanted to know how many militants there were. I answered, "those who know don't say and those who say don't know." The mayor countered: "Since there are so few of you guys, I guess the city is safe."

Among the four governors I served with, my favorites were Republicans Henry Bellmon and Frank Keating. Bellmon had demonstrated his mettle while serving as U.S. Senator. He defied his Oklahoma constituency and voted for the Panama Canal Treaty. When he returned to Oklahoma and became governor for a second time, he sided with Democrats in funding a landmark education reform bill. He stands out in my mind for taking down the Confederate flag and steadfastly refusing to cave under the pressure to resurrect it.

The very rightwing Republican Governor Keating was a favorite and the only white state official supporting reparations for riot survivors "if the state is found culpable." I am convinced a fellow Democrat would have ducked the issue. He also refused to fly the Confederate battle flag. After I retired, a Democrat governor, supported by all but one Black legislator, led the effort to hoist the Confederate national flag over the plaza of the Historical Society. Only Oklahoma and South Carolina have so honored Dixie.

During Keating's eight-year tenure, he never vetoed one of my bills. The governor and I had several confrontations publicly and privately, yet our disagreement on one issue never carried to the others. In one of our battles, Keating told the press I was wholly owned by the Democrats.

When a microphone was stuck in my face to respond, I fired back that "the governor should know that no Black has been owned since the Emancipation Proclamation." Later that evening, during a reception at the Governor's Mansion, he walked up to me scowling and responded to my comment to the press with, "Good shot," and shook my hand. We were friends until the next fight—and there were many.

Before reaching the political glass ceiling, I had also become the first African-American chairman of an appropriation subcommittee, with a budget of $900 million. I also served as secretary and chairman of the Oklahoma House's Democratic Caucus. The National Black Caucus of State Legislators (NBCSL) presented me with its highest award as the first lawmaker to complete the organization's

African-American agenda. Oklahoma was seen backward by the Black lawmakers and that view was changed. Tulsa was awarded the 1988 NBCSL convention.

In 1989, I was mistakenly involved in a legislative revolt that led to the ouster of Jim Barker as House Speaker. I was a member of a group of House members who called themselves "The Flaming Moderates." We often ate dinner together, discussing all the "what ifs" of the legislature and laughing at ourselves for our lack of political courage.

The fun group even had a flag, cool gray-colored with a yellow streak running through the middle. The deception disguised our more progressive leaning, our determined, forceful debates, and our tenacity to take on difficult issues.

The Flaming Moderates were certainly the winds behind my sails as I pushed the African-American agenda. Their courage was demonstrated when an Oklahoma Regent for higher education placed advertisements in several newspapers correctly calling Barker's leadership team "pork-barrel rednecks."

The speaker demanded an apology and threatened funding for Oklahoma colleges and universities if it was not forthcoming. The moderates submitted a letter to Barker urging him not to pursue the education funding cuts and observing that free speech was still the law of the land. My name was on the petition. I was attending a funeral and Larry Gish, a close buddy and seatmate, signed my name to the letter. He assumed I would have been on board.

I liked Barker. He had appointed me to my first chairmanship, secretary to the Democratic Caucus, slipped projects for my district onto the "pork-barrel list," and pushed the Senate into a $100,000 appropriation for Nation Black Caucus of State Legislators' national convention the year before. Had I been present, I would've risen up to my principles and said "no" to the protest letter.

I was the only Black in either house that held a leadership position on the all-important budget-writing committee where pork was dispensed. Barker's angry response was to remove the ten Flaming Moderates and the very innocent me off the budget committee. The moderates would have no hand in writing the budget. I was locked in. This was a group that had supported my agenda at every turn even though some of my controversial legislation had most always hurt them in their districts.

After several awkward lunches at the T-Bar Restaurant, I told the group the only answer was to oust Barker as speaker. We were not ready for that. Steve Lewis, a former Barker appropriation chairman, joined the group. Lewis planned to run for governor and was apparently seeking to find some distance from the unpopular Barker. We christened ourselves as the very clandestine "T-Bar 12" and named Lewis chairman. He pressed to attempt to oust Barker. The vote was unanimous among the now 14 members of the group.

The "T-Bar14" anticipated that if they signed up half of the Democrats, Republicans who hated Barker would join the legislative insurrection. After the necessary votes were reached, Rep. Dwayne Stidely of Claremore nervously rose and said, "Mr. Speaker, I move that Representative Jim Barker be removed as Speaker of the House of Representatives." I was still secretary of the Democratic caucus and was asked to take the gavel. I said no. All my requests were honored by Barker. I was a reluctant revolutionary.

Carolyn Thompson, my favorite and the most liberal member of the House, represented the University of Oklahoma district. She bravely slammed the petition on the desk and the rebellion was official. Barker's team was completely caught by surprise. The chamber filled as word spread and the pandemonium reached into all corners of the capitol.

The 72-25 vote was so complete, Republicans were not needed to decide the outcome. Lewis was elected Speaker. I am still embarrassed that this small dainty woman, Rep. Thompson, had the balls to do what I justcould not.

The story made the front-page headlines across the nation, measured in the same revolutionary tenor as Newt Gingrich's takeover of the Congress would be a few years later.

I'm not sure if it was punishment for my refusal to plant the ouster motion on the desk, or just an oversight as I was told, but my name was left off the budget-writing committee "by friends, T-Bar allies, and fellow Flaming Moderates." Moreover, the members of the

Black caucus supporting Barker shunned me. The relationship was never repaired with those serving during the ouster. How could I abandon Barker when he had done so much for me and other Black legislators? The truth that I had not signed the letter and how it really happened sounds like a lie, even to me. I only told Barker what had happened.

I raised hell about the oversight, adjustments were made, but I never felt good about the Flaming Moderates afterward and never again attended any of the celebratory meetings.

I was named Chairman of the Democratic Caucus and gained the initial funding for the construction of my beloved, pie-in-the-sky Greenwood Cultural Center. However, it didn't go unnoticed by me that as chairman of the caucus I was never invited into the leadership meeting, even though there were members who had no titles who were included.

I would forget my pride and turn my attention to gathering "pork" for my district with a new motto: "I'm agin' it if I ain't in it." With a lot of pushing, shoving, and trading, the dollars needed to construct the Greenwood Cultural Center were soon in place.

13
Riot Impact

The world breaks everyone, and some get strong in the broken places.
Ernest Hemingway

IN 1971, some friends and I organized *Impact Magazine* and published an issue highlighting the 50th anniversary of the 1921 Tulsa Race Riot. Ed Wheeler, a local history buff and radio commentator, approached me with a manuscript, rejected by the Tulsa Chamber of Commerce Magazine as too controversial. Wheeler was a crew-cut conservative and a general officer in the Oklahoma National Guard. *Impact Magazine* became the first media organization to offer the horrid account of those dark days. Few accounts of the riot are reported that don't refer to the magazine as one of its sources.

I was stunned by the reaction. After a television news channel broadcast a report based on the *Impact* story, the 2,500 copies of the magazine sold out immediately and a second and third printing sold as fast. This reaction surely spiked my interest in preserving this history and to attempt, one day, to do something about it. That day came after I was elected to the Oklahoma House of Representatives. In 1997, I filed a bill calling for $5 million in reparations for Tulsa's riot victims. The dollar figure was based on the same amount proposed by the legislature for the bombing of the Oklahoma federal building and for a national Indian museum.

In 1995, the nation watched in stunned reverence as bodies of men, women, and small babies were pulled from the nine-story Alfred P. Murrah Federal Building in Oklahoma City. The bombing claimed 168 lives and was called "the deadliest act of terrorism on U.S. soil." More accurately, the report should have noted it was the "second deadliest act." Until the 9/11 attack on New York's Twin Towers, the deadliest act of terrorism on American soil since the Civil War was the 1921 Tulsa Race Riot, when as many as 300 people were killed.

I supported the funding for all three projects. A friend had died in the bombing. I knew the treachery that forced the Five Civilized Tribes on the Trail of Tears. Indeed, my folks had come to Oklahoma with the Creek Indians as slaves and Freedmen on the Trail of Tears.

These tragedies should be commemorated. And I argued that victims of the 1921 Tulsa Race Riot should be so honored as well. Also, my position had been strengthened when, in 1994, the Florida legislature awarded cash payments to survivors of Rosewood, where 80 to 200 Blacks had been massacred in 1923.

My call for reparations in Tulsa for a race riot hidden from history drew national press attention, beginning with Bryant Gumbel on the *Today Show*. Tulsa's dirty little secret was exposed. The Tulsa riot was highlighted on *60 Minutes, Good Morning America, The Early Show, 20-20, CNN, the Washington Post, BET, New York Times, Dallas Morning News, Ft. Worth Star-Telegram, the Los Angeles Times, the Chicago Tribune*, and other media large and small including newspapers and television stations from London, Paris, Belgium and other foreign locations. A revision of history to include the virtually unknown Tulsa warfare was under way.

The $5 million in riot reparations seem tiny when the hell and the evil and the murder are weighed. Jim Hamilton, chairman of the appropriation committee, was convinced cash payments for riot survivors were unconstitutional. He agreed to support a legislative study. I accepted the compromise. The study was as much as I could have expected. Surprisingly, the media attention had parlayed into legislative impetus for the bill—even from the most conservative members of the Oklahoma House of Representatives.

When the bill came before the appropriation committee, I explained to members that the Black community destroyed by a race riot in Rosewood, Florida, would have amounted to a neighborhood in the Black Wall Street of America. There was more death and destruction in 1921 than during the Oklahoma City bombing. It was a tragic, infamous moment in Oklahoma and the nation's history. "As a consequence, our people suffered from a fatigue of faith," I told the lawmakers. "Some still are searching for a statute of limitations on morality, attempting to forget the longevity of the residue of injustice that at best can leave little room for the healing of the heart."

"Perhaps this study and subsequent humanitarian recovery events by the government and the good people of the state will extract us from the guilty and confirm the commandment of a good and just God.

"Our action can leave the deadly deeds of 1921 buried in this call for redemption, historical revision and repair," I said, "and hopefully with this study the feeling of the state will be quickened; the conscience of the brutal city will be ignited; the crimes against man and God will be denounced; the hypocrisy of the nation will be exposed, acknowledged and corrected.

I reiterated what abolitionist Frederick Douglass explained to a callous nation: "A government that can give liberty in its constitution ought to have the power to protect liberty, and impose civilized behavior in its administration."

The study, House Joint Resolution 1035, after litigious debate was passed by both houses of the legislature and signed into law by Gov. Keating. It created the *Oklahoma Commission to Study the 1921 Tulsa Race Riot.* Bob Blackburn, deputy director of the Oklahoma Historical Society, served as chairman. I recommended Scott Ellsworth, a former Tulsan, as the consultant historian. Ellsworth's book, *Death in a Promised Land,* was the definitive work on the Tulsa race riot. Historian and Tulsa native Dr. John Hope Franklin would serve as the commission's advisor.

In addition to Blackburn, white members were T.D. "Pete" Churchwell, president of a utility company; Abe Deutschendorf, a state representative; Jim Lloyd, attorney; and Robert Milacek, a state senator.

African-American members of the commission were Currie Ballad, a Black conservative and historian; Joe Burns, a riot survivor; Eddie Faye Gates, a retired public-school administrator and author; and history professors Dr. Vivian Clark and Jimmy White.

I had asked Ed Wheeler to serve on the commission. He had written the riot history for *Impact Magazine* in 1971. The conservative National Guard general refused. "I don't believe in reparations," he wrote. I read into his response that I was trying to stir things up; indeed I was. My terse response to him noted that I wanted the issue discussed and studied and a report written. Supporting reparations was not a prerequisite to serve on the commission. I didn't have the foggiest notion how many white members would support reparations. As it turned out, only one did.

Reparations for survivors and their descendants had no chance of passing the appropriation committee's scrutiny. To gain passage of the study, the $5 million for reparations was stripped from the bill. However, a section in the bill said: "The report may contain specific recommendations regarding whether or not reparations can or should be made and the appropriate methods to achieve the recommendations in the final report." This section became the focus of the study and caused havoc among commission members and in Tulsa's community, and stirred emotions nationally and internationally.

In a June 1, 2000, keynote address during Tulsa's commemoration of the riot at Mt. Zion Baptist Church, Dr. Franklin told the more than 2,000 gathered in the historic church (destroyed during the riot), that given the American taste for pseudo-salacious gossip, for intrigue, exploitation, and even for violence, it comes as no surprise that the belated public interest in the Tulsa riot outside the city invites a notoriety that the city doubtless feels is both undesired and undeserved.

"A veritable conspiracy of silence enveloped a considerable portion of the city," he said, noting that memories, science, and technology have improved our capacity to peer into the past.

"It is tempting to argue that the riot resulted from a long-planned conspiracy of white people to take over by violence certain choice lands and businesses owned by Black people," the historian pointed out. He said some facts are self-evident: That racial hatred and bigotry are so powerful, so full of evil, so venomous that they need no conspiracy or period of germination to do their destructive work. "The Sarah Page-Dick Rowland false incident was sufficient in itself to produce the terrible event," he added. "I hope with all my heart that the commission and the people of Tulsa will rise to their responsibility."

Dr. Franklin said reparations, whatever the amount, would be a mere pittance when compared with three quarters of a century of suffering by the victims of the looting, burning, bombing, and murder that so many endured.

Throughout the heavy lifting, when the riot bill was under consideration by the legislature or under attacks by its detractors, not one Black Tulsa church, minister, sorority, fraternity, or civic, civil rights, or social organization, or their leaders voiced a word in public or private support for the bill or for reparations. Matter of fact, Tulsa's Black newspaper, the *Oklahoma Eagle*, editorialized against reparations. Tulsa's Black community was silent and indifferent.

However. during and after the riot commission's deliberations, there were gangs of interested parties ready with rhetoric and criticisms. Interesting enough, I was speaking across the nation, updating other communities on the developments, but was never invited to talk anywhere at home.

Dr. Franklin had fired my interest in the Tulsa race riot as a young adult in high school and in later years. Our lives were somewhat connected. We were both Tulsa natives, attended Booker T. Washington High School, and were members of Christ Temple CME Church. The church had been destroyed during the race riot. Dr. Franklin's father, B.C. Franklin, an early member of Christ Temple, was a much-revered hero of the race war, and among the first Tulsa Blacks to become allied with the Democratic Party. Over the years the good doctor has tutored me in Oklahoma history and the African-American experience "from slavery to freedom."

"Whites wanted slavery or something closely akin to it. Blacks were not moving back to the plantation," was one of his blunt assessments. He said Greenwood was settled by Blacks who had been run out of everywhere. The first time I heard the word "reparations," it was from Dr. Franklin. I sheepishly asked what it meant. In near astonishment, he said, "Money, fool!"

14
Reparations Doomed

I will be as harsh as the truth and uncompromising as justice.
William Lloyd Garrison

THE FINAL REPORT of the Oklahoma Commission to Study the 1921 Tulsa Race Riot is a brilliant recollection of what likely happened during the riot and its aftermath. Historian Scott Ellsworth's account is outstanding, even compelling. It is laced with the methodical research of world-renowned forensic pathologist Clyde Snow. Dr. Snow uncovered the bones of Josef Mengele, the Auschwitz "Angel of Death" in Brazil and the victims of atrocities from Argentina to Ethiopia to Bosnia.

The study included scholarly work of Alfred L. Brophy, law professor and constitutional scholar. He assessed state and city culpability. It held an exceptional thesis by researchers Larry O'Dell on property loss, Richard S. Warner on the use of airplanes, and Robert L. Brooks and Alan H. Witten on mass grave locations.

From the beginning, there was discord among some commission members with Scott Ellsworth, the study's consulting historian. They charged him with being headstrong and insensitive to their views. Some viewed the study as more a vehicle for Ellsworth's self-promotion than a search for the truth. Ellsworth was thoroughly familiar with the records that survived the event. However, he never attempted to explain the limitations of oral history, and Black commissioners said he arrogantly dismissed the generations of renderings that framed the popular view of the riot among survivors.

Before Ellsworth began his work as consultant, I impressed on him and other commissioners significant details that should be included in any argument for reparations.

Clearly, if reparations were to be seriously addressed, three issues would have to be considered with recommendations: The constitutional bar that prohibits such payment; culpability of city, state, and county governments; and the statute of limitations on filing a lawsuit.

Shortly after the 1921 riot had broken out, a large number of whites—many of whom a while earlier were members of a would-be lynch mob—were sworn in as special deputies. The commission's report confirmed the city's action.

Major General Charles F. Barrett, in charge of the Oklahoma National Guard, wrote in his book, *Oklahoma After Fifty Years*, that the police chief had deputized 5,000 men and those deputies "were imbued with the same spirit of destruction that animated the mob."

I gave the commission members copies of minutes from the Tulsa City Commission following the riot. On June 7, 1921, six days after the riot, the mayor and city commissioners met. The City Commission's minutes documented "reimbursements" paid by the city throughout 1921 including:

Joe McGee, owner of a pawn shop, petitioned the commission for $3,994.57 for "guns and ammunition taken from his store on the night of June 1, 1921." In a unanimous vote, the commission paid McGee $2,151 "for guns and ammunition used on June 1, 1921." Dick Barton's pawn shop, Goldberg Loan Co., and Deluxe Cafe were paid claims "occasioned by reason of the riot on May 31 and June 1."

Mrs. C.A. Bankhead was paid $250.00 as owner of the building used as the colored library "and burned June 1, 1921". The City Commission paid Thomas Vickers "final action against the city for injuries and expenses sustained during the riot." Further, the city paid $125.00 for funeral expenses of Harry Roberts, who it confirmed "was killed in the recent riot."

My view was that those acts established culpability. Tulsa paid the pawn shops and others "reparations" or had purchased arms for the vigilantes called deputies. Funerals were banned for Blacks and at least thirteen were dumped in unmarked graves at city-owned Oaklawn Cemetery. Early in the deliberations, the commission's committee on reparations called for a nearly $35 million package, including $20,000 for each survivor. Opinion polls were taken, with unfavorable results. Newspaper editorials blasted the idea. Emotions were sizzling in the local media as radio shock jocks took to the airways in full assault on reparations.

State lawmakers complained and denounced the suggestion of cash payments. City Hall and legislative leaders became silent, not only on reparations, but on any talk of the riot. The public's reaction poisoned any discussions on the riot by policymakers. Nonetheless, several television documentaries served to keep the riot on the front burner of discussion.

Bob Blackburn, deputy director of the Oklahoma Historical Society, was the likely successor of the retiring director of the society. Perhaps feeling the heat from the riot controversy and that it might make his promotion problematic, Blackburn announced his opposition to reparations while speaking to a civic group and quietly resigned as the chairman. T.D. "Pete" Churchwell replaced him.

Ellsworth had his own ideas about the report, the nature of which was never clear to the commissioners, Blackburn, or me. He insisted that he didn't work for the commission or Blackburn, but naively asserted, "I work for the people of Oklahoma." In a dispute with Blackburn, Ellsworth asked me to intercede. I told him I had chosen not to sit on the commission, allowing it the full freedom to make decisions whether I agreed with them or not. My vision of the report was an update from his landmark work *Death in a Promised Land*. He said he was searching for something "new."

I may have thrown him toward "something new" when I told him a friend knew an elderly man in a nursing home who saw bodies buried near Sand Springs, a town sharing its western border with Tulsa. After several attempts, neither the elderly man nor his family wanted to talk.

Time was running out and I feared if the report was not completed within the year allotted, it would be shut down by the legislature. As the conflict between the riot panelists over reparations garnered headlines, Ellsworth was searching for "the something new"—the locations for mass graves, in every corner of the county—with the national media in full pursuit.

Ellsworth had not submitted a single sentence for the study. He had been paid more than $100,000 and surprisingly, Blackburn had not signed him to a contract outlining his responsibilities. The last straw came for me when Ellsworth settled on the city-owned Oaklawn Cemetery as the location of the mass graves. I met with the commission and called for the halt of the grave search. Ellsworth resisted and some commissioners wanted him fired.

I had known for years that Black victims of the riot were buried at Oaklawn in what Dr. Clyde Snow characterized as "cavalier, if not criminal, carelessness." The cemetery could have accounted for the official dead, but nowhere near the 300 alleged. When I learned Ellsworth demanded more money to complete the report and wanted the copyright in his name, I joined the chorus now singing loudly for his ouster. I asked Churchwell to allow me to search for a new historian. He told me to proceed but he wanted to see if Ellsworth's credibility with the commission, Blackburn, and me could be restored. The 900-pound gorilla in this battle was Dr. John Hope Franklin, Ellsworth's friend, mentor, and his former professor.

Churchwell met with Dr. Franklin in North Carolina and talked with Ellsworth on numerous occasions. The professor waded in on behalf of his former student. Black members of the commission had developed a heightened passion for dumping Ellsworth and further payment to him was unlikely to meet their approval. The commission was deadlocked. The deadline was approaching and the study appeared doomed.

To satisfy the legislative deadline and to request an extension, an interim report was hastily prepared calling for reparations. Blackburn said the commission decision to recommend reparations was based on the moral judgments that "our governments all fostered a climate of racial hatred. We're only saying for no other reason than that we need to do something," Blackburn explained.

Opposition to an extension was growing and passage would be difficult at best. However, Senator Maxine Horner and I were able to make the argument that no new state funds would be necessary. The extension passed the legislature. Then there was some intrigue.

Without warning, Governor Keating line-item vetoed the

measure in the last day of the session. A section of the bill provided $5 million "in the future" for a memorial. Keating thought it was to pay reparations before the final report was issued. A special session was called and the issue was placed on its agenda. Amid the chatter of radio shock jocks, the life of the commission was extended for "a year only."

The nearly 200-page report from the Oklahoma Commission to Study the Tulsa Race Riot of 1921 included recommendations, along with maps tracking the violence. I wrote the prologue, largely my remarks before the appropriations committee when the study was considered. The epilogue was written by Senator Maxine Horner.

Churchwell is the real hero and the primary reason any report exists. With state funds depleted, his corporate foundation offered funding to complete the report and pay Ellsworth.

Ellsworth was "contracted" to write a section of the report from the money raised by Churchwell and processed through the historical society. The other sections were written voluntarily by other experts. There was still resistance from the commissioners to working with Ellsworth.

It was at that point, Churchwell, with the support of the commission, approached and ultimately hired Dr. Danney Goble, a University of Oklahoma history professor, to compile the various research into a final report and serve as a barrier between Ellsworth and the commission.

Goble also had his difficulties, particularly with Black commissioners, and threatened to quit, only to be pulled back by Churchwell. The historian was openly against reparations and his summary all but avoided the issue. Another opportunity was lost.

Black commissioners and their one or two allies on the riot panel were in full revolt in pushing for reparation. The opposition was just as adamant. The report might have been completed as several "minority reports," but Churchwell insisted on a full agreement. The compromise came as unanimous support for the "concept of reparations." At the time, I told the *Dallas Morning News* I didn't think the commission addressed the issue of government culpability.

A few years before, Goble asked me to review a chapter to be included in his book, *Tulsa: The Biography of an American City*, with a section on the riot. The OU professor wrote that after the riot, when the Black-owned property immediately north of the railroad tracks lay in ruins, directors of the Tulsa Chamber of Commerce decided (as recorded in their official minutes) that "we must forget the cause of the riot and find a solution that is right." Goble argues the next sentence (in the Chamber's minutes) defines for the businessmen what was right: "We must determine whether this area is physically suited for a railroad terminal point."

Apparently, for the businessmen the site near Greenwood was okay. Goble noted that the Chamber swiftly adopted a resolution expressing it views:

> Whereas, the recent fire [1] in the northeast section of the city has made available a thoroughly feasible and practicable site for the Union Station and Joint Terminal,
>
> Now, therefore be it resolved, that it is the unanimous sentiment of the Chamber of Commerce and Federation of Allied Interest of Tulsa, Oklahoma, that the railroads and interurban of the city of Tulsa immediately take steps looking toward the erection of a Union Station and railroad and interurban terminal. ...

The Chamber pledged its unanimous and unqualified support for use of the charred area for the railroad station and gathered the united backing from the mayor and city commissioners. The Frisco railroad depot was completed a full ten years after the riot. "It took up most of what had been Greenwood's better residential and commercial district," Goble noted.

In 1921, the Greenwood area was zoned for industrial purposes and a restrictive fire ordinance was passed into law to prevent Blacks from rebuilding. Goble said the Chamber's plan entailed the building of cheap shacks "because when the proper time comes to condemn it, it will be possible to finance the proceedings."

Reparations Doomed

In 2007, Senator Maxine Horner and the Oklahoma Jazz Hall of Fame, allied with the Chamber and Tulsa's political establishment, purchased the railroad station and turned the facility back to the Black community as "The Jazz Depot."

As a result of the internal strife, the commission report was without a clear focus to offer policymakers, and other interested parties, a clear direction to follow and remedial actions to take.

The riot report notes that whites were stealing or "borrowing" weapons from the pawn shop. It doesn't mention the pawn shops were reimbursed by the City of Tulsa. It did include McGee's testimony that Tulsa police officers helped dole out the guns that were taken from his store.

There was Laurel Buck's admission that he was sworn in as a "Special Deputy," issued a weapon at a hardware store by police, and bluntly told by a law officer to "get a gun and get a nigger." He presumably proceeded to do just that. Dick Warner's research included in the reports, found a district court case where the St. Clair Oil Company (likely Sinclair Oil Company that owned one of two planes in the city) was accused by Black police officer Barney Cleaver of using its planes, "at the request and insistence of the city's agency," having carried Police Captain J.R. Blaine with others, and dropped turpentine balls and bombs on Greenwood. The case was dismissed without a response from the oil company or the city.

Professor Brophy emphasized in the report that Tulsa failed to protect its citizens and deputized the mob of "special deputies" who murdered Dr. A.C. Jackson, named by the famous Mayo brothers of Rochester, New York, as the most able Black surgeon in America. There is court testimony and eyewitness accounts of the cold-blooded murder of Dr. Williams, adding to an argument for culpability.

Judge John A. Oliphant testified in the trial of Police Chief John Gustafson. Oliphant was a prominent fixture in Tulsa political and civic life and close friends of both Mayor T.D. Evans and General Barrett. The retired 73-year-old magistrate offered eyewitness testimony on the behavior of the special deputies and the murder. He said the special deputies started fires instead of protecting property. Chief Gustafson was indicted, fined, found guilty, and fired for failure to take proper precautions for the protection of life and property.

Professor Brophy recorded that Judge Oliphant said Dr. Jackson emerged from his home with his hands raised saying, "Here I am. I want to go with you." Dr. Jackson was surrendering to several dozen armed men. The rogue special deputies shot him. The doctor was taken to the Convention Hall where he bled to death. The hall was set up as a concentration camp as Blacks were rounded up. Oliphant saw police officers and others who wore "badges or stars" burn Dr. Jackson's home.

Another argument: The special deputies were sworn in and armed by City Hall. Dr. Jackson was killed by its agents. There is no statute of limitations for murder.

I think a call by the commission to hold the city accountable for this murder would have driven that point home. Lawyers for the 1921 riot victims thought proving the city's culpability would be difficult, in view of the city's conviction and ouster of Police Chief John Gustafson for failure to protect life and property during the riot.

Other related information was presented by the commission's scholars, but was scattered throughout the report and was not correlated to effectively argue its recommendations.

The recommendations are only summarized in Churchwell's submittal letter, with ambiguous supporting rationales. They are in the report, but it requires a rigorous search and careful reading to find them..

In his opening remarks in the submittal letter, Churchwell listed several recommendations: direct payment to riot survivors and their descendants; a scholarship fund for students of the affected area; establishment of an economic development zone in the riot-torn district; and a memorial.

The study declared reparations to the historic Greenwood community in real and tangible form would be good public policy and "do much to repair the emotional and physical scars of this terrible incident in our shared past."

Sen. Horner and I had decided not to serve on the commission to avoid criticism from colleagues when we attempted to implement its recommendations. I now think that was a strategic mistake. Had the two of us served on the commission, we could have insisted on crafting a recommendation for changing the constitution to allow cash payment and perhaps drawn media attention to the issue.

The attorney general's staff had advised us that reparations were constitutionally prohibited. The state "couldn't make loans or donations by gift to any individual" without a contract for services rendered. Afterwards, we couldn't garner any support among lawmakers for such a change in the state's constitution.

Prior to the report presentation at the state capitol on February 21, 2001, I said to commission members, "Today is not for grandstanding." I said that we needed to learn what commitments would be publicly made by the political leaders. I specifically said to Eddie Faye Gates, a more expressive and media-conscious member of the commission, "This is not your day." She agreed.

With a horde of local and national media present, before the governor, House Speaker and Senate President Pro Tempore could make any commitment to "do something," Mayor Susan Savage asserted that survivors were not asking for reparations.

Mrs. Gates interrupted and took over the news conference. She said the mayor's statement was untrue—that survivors deserved and demanded reparations. This intrusion shattered any possibility for firm commitments from legislative leaders on anything and the Gates declaration became the riot news of the day. Governor Keating had told me he supported reparations "if the state was shown to be culpable" and he was prepared to say as much during the news conference. However, the press centered on Mrs. Gates' comments and, in the commotion, policymakers eased out of the room. The battle to secure reparations was presented and lost on the same day.

After two years of bickering, brawling, and research, Ellsworth had completed what turned out to be a more scholarly adaptation of his book. He held a commitment from Churchwell that his work could not be changed, edited, or added to. His writing was not coordinated with and held none of the information gathered by the commissioners.

Even so, the final report is unrivaled to any other news account's, book's, or documentary's portrayal of the Tulsa terrorism. Was it worth it? The answer is a resounding yes!

After the news conference, Senator Horner and I successfully passed legislation establishing a scholarship program and a bill to place an enterprise zone in the affected area. The legislature also agreed to $5 million for a design committee to develop a museum and memorial. Perhaps more important is that the incident is now branded into the national consciousness.

Was it enough?

I am convinced had it not been for the Oklahoma City bombing of the Murrah Federal Building at this intersection of history, the media and a very conservative Oklahoma legislature would never have considered a riot study or $5 million in funding for its recommendations.

Finally, the riot study commissioners could have initiated a call for reparations to be raised privately and also for a lawsuit to be filed if such redress wasn't properly considered.

The commission's report, even with its flaws, exposes future generations to the 1921 riot and a likely version of what happened. Before the report, the riot was only discussed in hushed tones, and communicated about in different—and sometimes contradictory ways—from Black and white perspectives.

After the GOP took over the legislature, the final payment for the commission of nearly $2 million was dropped from the budget. Tulsa's Black legislators, Senator Judy Eason-McIntyre and Representative Jabar Shumate, were silent at the legislative action. The city, including the two African-Americans serving on the City Council, Joe Williams and Roscoe Turner, also said nothing.

Tulsa and the entire state have conducted a seminar in silence regarding the riot. Perhaps Black leaders were swayed by the lyrics of a song written by Beatle George Harrison: *When you don't know where you're going, every road takes you there.*

In my view, any cash payment related to the massacre had to be raised privately.

I had met John Gaberino a year before during some difficult negotiation about the future of historically Black Langston University's presence in a five-university consortium in Tulsa. Gaberino, a well-respected utility company executive, was board chairman of the Metropolitan Tulsa Chamber of Commerce. Senator Maxine Horner, who had sponsored the riot study in the state Senate, and I met with him and discussed reparations and other issues centered on the riot.

Gaberino was familiar with the Chamber's 1921 commitment to rebuild Greenwood and pay reparations "to the last penny." He agreed to call together a group of corporate leaders and begin a fundraising effort.

We set a figure of at least $5,000 for each of the nearly 200 survivors. One million dollars or more was the goal. Gaberino was convinced that the money could be raised and agreed to convene some of the most influential business leaders in the city. Senator Horner and I were to invite Black leaders to the meeting. Before the meeting was set, Gaberino had raised $200,000 and the Oklahoma Legislative Black Caucus contributed $15,000.

Then, political shenanigans challenged the meeting's success. Williams, the Black city councilman, refused to attend. Even though the meeting had never been announced publicly, he said he would not attend because "his constituents" opposed collaboration with the Chamber. Williams, Senator Horner, Roscoe Turner (the other Black city councilor, who did attend the session), and I represented the Black community that included the 35-block area burned in the riot. Unlike Williams, we hadn't been under any such pressure from our mutual constituents.

And there was another problem. My aggressive stance against an anti-union "right-to-work" law became an issue for some of the Chamber leaders. I had called right-to-work the Chamber's "woolly booger" of exploitation and said the business group wanted workers to compete with Bangladesh for wages.

At the meeting, Ruben Gant, the president of the Black Chamber of Commerce, said the sum of merely $5,000 was an insult to the survivors. I complained to him that my aunt was a survivor and had never had, at one time, more than $200 in her life. She would be very pleased. That didn't sway his objection and other Blacks were silent. The mood of the meeting changed. This effort was being effectively derailed.

Complicating the drive for reparations even more: The mayor's office had contacted Gaberino and told him that any public discussion on reparations would jeopardize a critical vote on a sales tax extension due before the public in a couple of weeks.

Nonetheless, in a bold statement a week before the sales tax vote, Gaberino said the Chamber would work toward implementing a number of proposals "including reparations." The Chamber chairman was the first Tulsa voice declaring such support for the study's recommendation and compensation for survivors. The *Oklahoma Eagle,* with a circulation largely limited to the Black community, was the only media to report Gaberino's announcement.

The Chamber chairman was speaking before nearly 2,000 persons, many of whom were legislators and business and community leaders, at an event honoring riot survivors. His announcement had no effect on the $390 million sales tax extension. It passed overwhelmingly.

Actress Alfre Woodard, a Tulsa native, delivered the banquet address. She said generations of Tulsa's Blacks and whites were still affected by the events of the riot and its aftermath.

The state offered $750,000 as the first stage of a $5 million commitment to build a museum and memorial. Mayor Susan Savage made strong commitments "to do something," then retreated to ignoring the riot. After some chastisements near the end of her term of office, she submitted a $1.5 million package to the City Council for the land and the John Hope Franklin Reconciliation Museum. The two Black city councilmen led the charge that defeated the proposal.

Roscoe Turner told me he wanted an Indian museum, even though the world-class Gilcrease Museum bordered his district and the state was planning a massive complex in Oklahoma City. State Sen. Kelly Haney, also a Seminole tribal member, told me the Indian museum had first been offered to Tulsa and turned down by the mayor.

The proposed $18 million Franklin museum was to be constructed in Joe Williams' district. Williams led a group who saw themselves as the political Godfathers of the Black community. He and his cohorts used the presidency of the NAACP to launch themselves as political candidates. In addition to Williams, two other NAACP presidents ran for the office I held.

Williams may have been hounded by the "reparations or nothing" crowd and may have also thought funding for the project would enhance my reelection. Unknown to me, he and his allies were preparing to field a candidate against me. While I'm a life member and former board member of the NACCP, only the few in their clique knew when or where the meetings were held. After I retired, Williams sought my former position. Sen. Horner and I recruited a candidate and Williams was convincingly beaten by a relatively unknown candidate who had only recently moved back home.

About this time, a countywide bond issue was planned. It was proposed that the riot museum and memorial be included.

Before the discussions could grab hold, a local reparation coalition convinced Harvard University's Professor Charles Ogletree, Jr., to sue the city and state for reparations on behalf of riot survivors in federal court. The Harvard law professor is one of the nation's best-known constitutional lawyers.

I served with Ogletree on the Washington, D.C.-based Trans-Africa organization's committee on U.S. reparations, headed at the time by Randall Robinson. Ogletree and Johnny Cochran (Michael Jackson and O.J. Simpson's famed trial attorney) also served on the national reparations committee. Ogletree pulled together a dream team of attorneys and scholars that included Cochran and Dr. Franklin.

To overcome the statute of limitations, the federal lawsuit alleged the state's riot report extended the time. Some critics and radio shock jocks said the extension allowing court action was my underlying reason for the report. I wish I could claim such brilliance.

After the lawsuit was filed, the Chamber of Commerce, Mayor Bill LaFortune, the City Council, and County Commissioners were convinced the riot measures could hurt, or worse, defeat the bond issue. They were not included. The bond issue passed and so did interest in the riot. I took the lead in raising $75,000 in private funds to construct a ten-foot granite headstone that recorded the known deaths and businesses destroyed. *The Black Wall Street Memorial* became the only symbol in the city acknowledging the Tulsa race riot.

Scott Ellsworth, the historian I recommended to the commission as its consultant, became my critic, in James S. Hirsch's book, *Riot and Remembrance*. Ellsworth found fault in my writing the preamble to the commission report describing the riot's place in history. There wasn't any notice taken that I was asked to write the essay by the Greenwood Cultural Center's board. Ellsworth also complained about my rhetoric in describing my anger as one of the legacies of the riot.

What I meant was that the anger was handed down from generation to generation. Hirsch claimed Ellsworth and I feuded because we each felt an ownership of the riot story. That's not so. I freely admit Ellsworth is the expert on the Tulsa race riot and its most passionate scholar. Our distance came when I refused Ellsworth's telephone calls after I tired of his self-serving shenanigans when the deadline was approaching and completing the report became critical.

Again, there isn't anybody who knows the riot's official history as thoroughly as Ellsworth. He is an excellent scholar, researcher, writer, and PR man. All that talent is funneled into one gargantuan ego that may be rivaled by my own. My high school history professor claimed that early Black Tulsans "didn't take no shit" and neither did I.

The Hirsch book also served my Mama with an injustice. Hirsch sent me the galley that identified former Tulsa University Professor Nancy Feldman as saying my mother could not buy me a suit or nice shoes on my high school graduation.

"So, the principal's wife took him to see several sympathetic white Tulsans and asked for contributions. The money came in," Hirsch reported Dr. Feldman said, and that I wore a fine "sharkskin suit" and black shoes for my graduation. I told Hirsch that story was untrue and indeed I had not known the principal's wife when I graduated high school. I grew up in segregated North Tulsa. When I graduated high school in 1959, the only whites I knew were "the bootlegger" and the Lebanese owner of what we called the "Jew" store.

I was more fashion-conscious than Hirsch offered me credit for.

Sharkskin was old men's clothing; no young Black of my generation would be buried in that "shiny" shit. In fact, my mama bought me and my best friend identical dark blue suits. She kept more than a few dollars under her mattress.

I worked after school and bought my own Stacy Adams shoes. Mama operated a resale store and I owned several suits that would have been just fine for graduation. Mama may turn in her grave with the notion that some rich do-gooder had to dress her son.

Further, I only knew the principal's wife, Thelma Whitlow, from her fine reputation in the community as head of the YWCA. Years later, Mrs. Whitlow and I became friends and she served as my campaign manager in my election to the Oklahoma House of Representatives in 1982.

Dr. Feldman's name was removed from the attribution when the book was published.

I first met Dr. Feldman sometime after 1963 when I returned home after serving in the Air Force. We met after a disagreement over her expert testimony in the trial of a Black Panther arrested for cursing during an anti-war rally. I was involved in the case and had recruited the Panther's lawyer.

As I remember, her argument was that Black obscenity was angry protest language germinating from poor education. I said it was all that and more, and regardless of education, if an obscenity was preceded by a positive adjective, indeed the obscenity was to be taken positively. She disagreed.

The case was won in the U.S. Supreme Court and I later studied it in law school.

Even though I explained to Hirsch my differences with Ellsworth and Dr. Feldman's story of the "sympathetic" white woman, I suspect their version made better copy.

Hirsch accused me of wearing the Chai, a Jewish symbol of life, to attract Jewish voters. I'm not aware of any Jews residing in the majority Black legislative district. I bought the jewelry in Israel and didn't know it meant anything until I read it in his book.

With that off my chest, I can return to other preaching.

Before my retirement in 2002, the fabric of the state's affirmative action programs, my major priority in the legislature, was unraveling. Nearly all programs combating discrimination were under all-out attack by the courts and the increasingly conservative Oklahoma lawmakers.

At least four lawsuits accused the state of reverse discrimination and Attorney General Drew Edmondson chose to settle each of them, paying off the complainers. Racism was again profitable.

15
Blacks Salute Confederacy

Black people have always been a commodity subject to barter from white people for their own needs and self-interest.
                                                            Derrick Bell

ONE OF THE MORE OMINOUS signals of retreat and complete abandonment of African-American civil rights goals, accomplishments, and aspirations came after my retirement from the Oklahoma legislature. Black lawmakers commanded the withdrawal.

My son Kavin is a history buff. On visiting the capitol, he asked me why the Confederate flag was prominently flowing near the front entrance, inasmuch as Oklahoma was not part of the Deep South states. I hadn't noticed, didn't know, and asked the Oklahoma History Society to research the issue. The society did not know when or why the racist symbol was planted there.

I was told by Henry Bellmon, Oklahoma's first Republican governor, that in 1966 he had authorized flying the Confederate banner and that of 13 other "nations" that had held "dominion" over the territory at some time. The flag display had been part of the Oklahoma exhibit presented during the New York World's Fair in 1964.

I requested an Attorney General's opinion to determine if the rebellious South was considered a "nation" and if the so-called battle flag could represent it. The basis for flying the star and bars was tied to the Civil War. As federal troops withdrew from Indian Territory, the Five Civilized Tribes fought for the Confederacy and therefore the law assumed that the South had held dominion over the territory.

On July 2, 1987, Attorney General Robert Henry, a former member of the legislature and fellow member of the "Flaming Moderates," handed down an opinion declaring that since the Confederacy was never legally recognized as a separate and independent nation, it could not be considered as having "held dominion" over Oklahoma and a Confederate flag could not be displayed on any state property. He also based his ruling upon a U.S. Supreme Court edict that "a doctrine of secession is a doctrine of treason."

Attorney General Henry noted the flag could be hoisted if authorized by the state. He also explained that there were four different Confederate flags and that the "battle flag" flown over the capitol was never formally adopted. The South's official flag was white with the battle flag's star and bars in the upper right corner.

I immediately sent correspondence to Governor Bellmon, who had returned as chief executive after a stint in the U.S. Senate, citing "great anguish" with the public display of the Confederate symbol and requested that the governor issue an executive order removing it. He refused, claiming it was part of the state's history.

At the time, battle flags were flown at the capitol in Alabama, Oklahoma, Florida, Georgia, Louisiana, Mississippi, and South Carolina. In these states, to burn the American or Confederate flag held the same criminal penalty. State flags of Florida, Georgia, and Mississippi have Confederate symbols built into their designs.

I filed a bill to snatch the flag from the capitol. It failed by seven votes. The nation's first attempt to remove official sanctioning of the battle flag caused an angry firestorm from Blacks and whites. I've been threatened for my political views before, but never as much as from the calls and letters that came after my assault on the old Confederacy.

In the middle of the media flurry, Governor Bellmon and I met on the issue. The governor said a solution had been found and asked me not to mention it to the mass of news reporters waiting outside his office.

The governor's director of the Office of Public Affairs, Helen Arnold, orchestrated the solution. I knew Arnold from the 1960s as an iron-willed supporter of civil rights and the African-American community. A former Republican legislator from Tulsa, she was considered too liberal and was ousted by a Baptist minister. Later, that minister became as liberal as Arnold.

The Office of Public Affairs was in charge of the capitol grounds and maintained the flag plaza. During a renovation project, Arnold ordered the dismantling of the flag display. The Confederate flag now was a part of the distant history it represented.

But the rebellion would return. Rebel disciples, some in full Confederate regalia, visited the capitol and stood outside my office demanding the restoration of the "symbol of southern heritage." The only way I could remove them from my front door was to ask them in to talk. They would quietly leave.

With Bellmon's adamant support, Arnold steadfastly refused to reinstall the flag. State Senator Herb Rozelle, claiming his ancestors fought for the South, passed a resolution ordering that the flag plaza be restored and the Stars and Bars be reinstated.

The flag plaza was re-erected. Thirteen of the original 14 flags were raised again. Absent was the Confederate battle flag. When the senator demanded that the flag be posted without delay, Arnold responded that Rozelle's resolution didn't specify which flag was to be raised and none would be displayed until the clarification was made in law.

A committee of Oklahoma historians and Civil War buffs were gathered to study the issue. They wrote a report that recommended that the Stars and Bars would be an appropriate flag to fly.

Bellmon and Arnold ignored the report.

Rozelle and I battled almost daily in the press. I considered the senator as somewhat of a moderate and was a bit shaken from his fierce insistence on re-fighting the Civil War. As a Cherokee, a tribe practicing slavery, he too was a relic of the Old South.

I wrote to Rozelle that our fight was divisive and we both suffered from different ancestral viewpoints. "What is a symbol of heritage to you is a reminder of slavery and lynching to me," I said. Rozelle represented Tahlequah, Oklahoma, the capital of the Cherokee Nation. However, former House Speaker Bill Willis, who represented the area in the House of Representatives, voted to remove the flag. He was Cherokee also and caught hell from his constituents for doing so.

Rozelle sought a compromise. He offered to substitute it with the last banner approved by the Confederacy. I said that symbol was even worse. The South's official flag would leave Oklahoma sanctioning what the attorney general had cited as a treasonous rebellion. It would be accepting the South as a nation. Nowhere outside that South had that been done.

He told me he would move a new flag bill through the legislature and he threatened to initiate legal action against Arnold for ignoring his first resolution.

I was invited to express my opinion in a *Point of View* column for the *Tulsa World,* Tulsa's leading newspaper. I wrote: "to satisfy the inherent racism let the Stars and Bars be raised, let it be branded in our hearts and souls. Let it replace our sensitivity, define our humanity and let it speak for our common sense. We are what we are."

A month later, the newspaper reversed an earlier position and editorialized: "The Flag fuss: Enough," and said it was time for someone to back off. "Is it sufficient to antagonize a substantial number of our citizens? ... We don't think so."

As the controversy continued, the *Tulsa World* said in a later editorial that "if the effect is to create hostility and conflict, why bother." Still, the heated debate lingered. The evening paper, the *Tulsa Tribune,* widely blamed for triggering the 1921 Race Riot in its news account, editorialized in favor of keeping the flag.

Bob Cullison, President Pro Tempore of the Senate, was an old friend from Skiatook near Tulsa. I told him I was prepared to shut down the capitol in protesting Rozelle's effort. I had been speaking with and gathering support from university students and church and civil rights groups all over the state.

Surprisingly Cullison found the flag objectionable and said he would talk with Rozelle, who was a member of his leadership team. Sometime later at a legislative reception, Rozelle approached me and said he would no longer pursue the issue. We shook hands. Our rhetorical battle was over. The Confederacy at long last had surrendered—or had it?

After Bellmon, David Walters became governor. While campaigning, Walters asked for my support. I said yes, conditioned on his signing a letter stating unequivocally that the Confederate flag would never fly over state property and that he would veto any bill and halt any administrative effort to post the flag. I wrote the letter. Walters signed the pact.

No sooner than he was in office, the flag battle was on again. Paula Hern replaced Arnold as director of the Office of Public Affairs, the department in charge of the state facilities, and as such she inherited the flag fuss. Hern suggested flying the rebels' official flag, as Rozelle had pushed earlier.

Unacceptable.

I sent her the attorney general's opinion, news clippings from the earlier fights and the letter signed by Walters stating that he would never fly Stars and Bars over the capitol. I then met with the governor. Walters said the agreement would be kept. The Confederate flag would not be raised.

In 1993, Alabama followed Oklahoma and won a lawsuit to remove the Confederate symbols. In 2000, South Carolina removed the Stars and Bars from the state capitol's rotunda and installed it next to a monument honoring fallen Confederate soldiers. The compromise satisfied no one and the NAACP launched a national boycott against the state. Florida quietly removed the southern Civil War symbol in 2001.

After Walter's term, Republican Governor Frank Keating settled the issue quickly. He said publicly that he considered the flag a racist symbol and it would not be raised during his administration. The Claremore chapter of Sons of Confederate Veterans lost an appeal to the Oklahoma Supreme Court to restore the flag.

We had won.

Or maybe not.

Kevin Cox, an African-American state representative from Oklahoma City, held a reputation for outrageously shooting from the hip and browbeating those who found themselves on his "shit list." On one occasion, he called the director of corrections a "liar, thief and thug" on the House floor. He was forced to apologize or face slander charges.

During my first effort to tear down the flag, Cox expressed indifference during Black Caucus discussions on the Confederate issue.

Nonetheless, he vehemently argued for the bill and refused to sign on to the Rozelle compromise proposal of flying the South's official flag.

Later, on an Oklahoma City radio station, Cox condemned the attempt to raise the flag and said Jefferson Davis, the Confederate president, should have been put to death for treason.

After my retirement, Cox continued "fat mouthing" on the flag and attracted the ire of Oklahoma City's rightwing press. I suspect he was stampeded into offering a concession to the local rebels.

He filed a bill allowing any flag removed from the flag plaza of the Oklahoma State Capitol Building to be transferred to the Oklahoma Historical Society. Unbelievably, Cox was now advocating waving the Stars and Bar within the Capitol complex. Cox—the outspoken militant who had worked so hard to close the first debate, and said no to Rozelle's offer, he who would have hanged Davis—now sought to honor the Confederate president's treason by flying the South's lynching cloth.

The Oklahoma City Democrat aligned himself with the most vociferous, rightwing proponent of the flag, who had spent years keeping the issue alive. Senator Maxine Horner was left out of the loop: Rep. Judy Eason-McIntyre, Rep. Opio Toure, and Sen. Angela Monson, along with Cox—four of the five members of the Black Caucus—orchestrated the dastardly deed of fighting for the South's most important symbol of the Lost Cause.

The bill unanimously passed the House of Representatives, without debate and in almost conspiratorial silence. The battle flag was set to be flown at the new Oklahoma History Center. Senator Monson, an African-American from Oklahoma City, became its principal author in the Senate, where the battle flag was substituted for the official Confederate standard.

The bill would have moved through the Senate also without debate had Senator Horner not raised an objection "to this shameful relic identified with slavery."

Monson said Oklahoma was not only the first state to remove the flag, "it's now the first state to replace it." Oklahoma became the first and only state to officially sanction the Confederacy as a nation.

Oklahoma, led by Black lawmakers, had endorsed the rebellion of the Old South.

Monson noted that the debate had begun 15 years ago and said the bill presents a "sensible and appropriate compromise." She said the lawmakers were acknowledging that part of history.

Governor Brad Henry, the cousin of Robert Henry, the attorney general who issued the opinion banning the flag, signed the bill into law. Oklahoma and South Carolina stand alone in such adoration.

Senator Horner retired and Representative Eason-McIntyre sought that Senate seat. During her campaign she was chastised by opponents for voting to support the reinstallation of the Confederate flag. The last weekend before the vote, she inundated the airways with radio commercials erroneously denying the charge that was indeed true. Her lie was believed and she was elected.

During my 20 years in the Oklahoma legislature, among my proudest political triumphs was my role in decommissioning the damnable rag from the capitol, the first in the nation to do so, and seeing several others follow Oklahoma's lead.

My most depressing moment is that the flag is back, placed there with the active support of African-American lawmakers. The punishment for hypocrisy is long-term memory, and the Confederate flag flying in the shadow of the state capitol provides for that.

Oklahoma history is often presented as Boomers and Sooners, on horseback and in covered wagons, opening the prairie. It is seen as oil fields pumping the liquid gold into an insatiable nation's lifeline. Oklahoma has had its glory days. It is also the state where all of its 77 counties voted against Barack Obama for president of the United States.

There are those who would include the Civil Wars years and fighting for the Confederacy as part of Oklahoma's pioneering spirit. But that fails to consider that this symbol is a powerful and painful reminder of the 750,000 dead, many of whom died to prevent this flag from controlling America. The flag represents a refusal to recognize a common destiny that makes us all a proud and united people.

Perhaps the South's inhumanity and the immorality of its cause is precisely why the Confederates lost the war. Oklahoma's preservation of the racist banner is a lingering victory for Dixiecrats. Oklahoma is now a part of promoting the Old South's rejuvenation, without recognizing or caring that symbols in themselves can be oppressive.

16
Memorial Without Eulogy

The forces of hate and violence must not be allowed to gain their victory, not just in our society, but in our hearts.
    The Reverend Billy Graham, prayer service after the Oklahoma City bombing

DESPITE ROADBLOCKS from powerful whites, after the massacre Black Tulsans almost immediately began rebuilding their community in wood, brick and stone, according to a report on Christmas Eve 1921 by Dr. Maurice Willows, relief director of the Red Cross. He said it demonstrated Black people's ability to make progress against the most cunningly planned opposition.

The Oklahoma Commission to Study the Tulsa Race Riot estimated losses of $16 million in today's dollars. The State agreed to a $5 million funding package, leaving an $11 million shortfall. In 2003, my Aunt Mildred Evitt Wilburn, born the year of the riot, was among the 150 survivors who instigated a federal lawsuit against the City of Tulsa and the State of Oklahoma for compensatory damages resulting from the riot.

Harvard law professor Charles Ogletree, Jr., leading a distinguished team of attorneys, filed the suit, *Alexander v. Governor of Oklahoma*, in the Northern district of Oklahoma. Ogletree also served as counsel for the Reparations Coordinating Committee, seeking reparations for the "contemporary victims of slavery and the century-long practice of *de jure* racial discrimination which followed slavery [and segregation]." He called Tulsa "ground zero" for reparations advocates.

The federal lawsuit scattered white political support as fast as the machine guns positioned on Standpipe Hill during the riot scattered Black residents. Even the Black politicians were running. And just as rapidly, any healing offered by the Metropolitan Tulsa Chamber of Commerce, if not mortally wounded, was bleeding badly.

Before the lawsuit, nearly $3 million of the $5 million in state funding was in an account for riot-related projects. An architect was hired to begin the planning for the John Hope Franklin Museum of Reconciliation, which was never built. A world-class sculptor was commissioned and completed "The Tower of Reconciliation," a 30-foot bronze depiction of riot scenes; a companion structure symbolically highlights the "Hate, Harshness, Humiliation and Hope," with larger-than-life human figures. Both were drawn from my research and recommendation.

Sidewalk plaques were placed along the historical boulevard noting the location of businesses lost during the two-day war.

The riot scholarship program restricted to Tulsa was funded for $300,000 by the State Regents for Higher Education. The reconciliation scholarships are now available in addition to the statewide Oklahoma Higher Learning Access Program sponsored by Senator Horner, who also sponsored the other riot-related legislation. The legislature has pumped more than $100 million into the grants, now called Oklahoma's Promise. According to the regents, it remains an ongoing struggle to maintain Black student involvement in both programs.

At the time of the survivors' lawsuit, there was also serious discussion about placing the additional funding needs of the museum and memorial in a proposed countywide bond issue. The day the lawsuit was filed, radio shock jocks imposed themselves into the riot debate and shut down what little support existed for the ideas. The lawsuit had come a bit untimely for Tulsa's goodwill and the bond issue passed without addressing the riot.

There were disingenuous promises by Mayor Bill LaFortune and others "to raise the money privately." However, Tulsa Metropolitan Ministries was the only group that remained focused on the riot and distributed over $20,000 in donations to the survivors.

African-American elected officials also turned the page on the riot. City Councilor Roscoe Turner and newly elected Councilor Jack Henderson hid from riot-related discussions. I had defeated

Henderson in a landslide on two occasions when the riot issue was before the legislature.

Equally troubling, state Sen. Judy Eason-McIntyre and Rep. Jabar Shumate never requested the funding and have shown no support for riot-related funding or long-established funding programs in the district. Engaging the issues of the riot appears to be as embarrassing to these leaders as it is for the white power structure. It was a funeral without a eulogy.

Meanwhile, two years after riot-related funding was removed, the mayor proposed and constructed a $10 million baseball facility directly across the street from where the museum was planned.

In February 2003, the survivors, Ogletree, and his team of lawyers appeared before a federal court in Tulsa to argue the case of reparations for the Tulsa victims. A federal judge ruled the statute of limitations in the case had expired and the suit should have been filed in the 1960s, when the survivors had an opportunity of being treated fairly and without fearing retaliation based on racism.

The appeal was lost and the U.S. Supreme Court refused to hear the case. Ogletree said courts are reluctant to award damages for actions that occurred far in the past.

The plaintiffs took their uphill battle to the Congress in April 2007. The House Judiciary Committee held a hearing on a bill by its chairman John Conyers. Conyer's bill would lift the statute of limitations and allow the survivors to re-file their lawsuit. The Michigan Congressman said evidence suggested that governmental officials deputized and armed the mob that stormed the Black Wall Street of America.

During the hearing, Dr. John Hope Franklin retold his riot recollections and Dr. Olivia Hooker, six years old at the time, said her mother told her, "Your country is shooting at you." She said that was disturbing to her and she wondered why her country would be trying to kill her. Mrs. Hooker's father, S.D. Hooker, owned a "high class" haberdashery on Greenwood and lost more than $45,000 in the destruction.

While Black property loss was unofficially set at $1.5 million by Chamber and city officials, Mrs. Hooker's father, chairman of the

East End Relief Committee, representing the Black community's interest, declared that after the riot the city published a notice that it would restore "$4 million" in lost property owned by Blacks. The much-revered Red Cross relief director Maurice Willows also said the damage would "easily reach the $4 million" and noted the figure was "conservative." The *Kansas City Star* reported the same amounts in losses. In a *Chicago Defender* interview on August 8, 1921, Hooker said there was no pretense (by the Chamber or the city) toward keeping its word. "The Tulsa Bar Association has even gone as far as to give an opinion freeing the city of all liability in connection with the great conflagration."

Even with the setbacks and as disappointed as they were, my Aunt Mildred and the other Tulsa race riot survivors never dreamed that their plight and the 1921 carnage would ever reach a federal court, let alone become an issue for national discussion.

Meanwhile, the long-simmering feud between Blacks and Native Americans erupted. Later the racial explosion reached the halls of Congress, as the Cherokee Nation attempted to completely evict nearly 3,000 Blacks from the tribe.

Similar disenfranchisements were employed before the Civil War and settled by treaty afterward. With the defeat of the Confederacy, all existing treaties with the five tribes were scrapped. They were squeezed into 20 million acres and the treaty of 1866 imposed a stipulation that "all freedmen who have been liberated by voluntary act of their former owners or by law, as well as all free colored persons who were in the country at the commencement of the rebellion, and are now residents therein, or who may return within six months, and their descendants, shall have all the rights of native[s]." And further, that regulations or rules the tribe adopted "which bear oppressively" on any citizen of the nation and "discriminating" against any and all are "prohibited and void."

The Chickasaw and Choctaws still hold hostility toward Freedmen, opposing tribal membership despite the 1866 treaty. In 2001, the Creek Nation changed its membership to require Indian blood. The court ruled against the Nation, but Black members are still denied benefits. Seminole Blacks won a legal battle in 2003, but without benefits. Freedmen have been locked in battle with the tribe to gain access to $56 million awarded to the tribe by the federal government.

The U.S. Department of the Interior oversees Indian affairs and is "reviewing" the legality of dumping Black Cherokee tribal members. U.S. Representative Diane Watson pressed a bill through Congress that would remove federal funding for the tribe and suspend tribal authority to operate a casino, exposing the Cherokees to lawsuits in non-Indian courts. The Freedmen's war with the Five Civilized Tribes could raise a legal precedent.

If the federal government can impose payments and land allotments to former slaves from the tribes, reparations for Deep South's slaves may also be due. Author William Loren Katz describes the action more clearly in *Black Indians: A Hidden Heritage*:

> The U.S. Government and white citizens had once demanded Native Americans adopt slavery and hunt runaways. Now they demanded that all slaves of Indians become free and equal. The white man had again spoken with forked tongue and, as always, in his own interest.
>
> In the meantime, there is a Cherokee casino in the Tulsa area and others scattered across Northeastern Oklahoma. The same is so for other tribes throughout the state. Blacks aren't boycotting the slot machines protesting the tribal actions, perhaps not knowing or, more seriously, not caring that recent anti-Black powwow sums up the historical character of The Five Civilized Tribes.

Regarding the riot? For the moment my feelings about the languishing mission are no longer focused on the white community as they were for many years before the study. The African-American community has surpassed whites' ongoing and systemic denial on the issue. Black leaders are now the principal conspirators in maintaining the silence. If not for the noise created by Professor Ogletree and his high-quality lawyers, there would be no sound at all.

I wish I could report that the historical journey I have traveled has made Tulsa's African-American legacy more comforting and complete. I cannot. It remains unfinished business.

For me, this struggle up the mountain top tested the very core of the definition of who we are as Blacks and whites, and the difficulty in securing and maintaining allies who, when challenged, are not distracted from the decency of justice. Things can change, but it's less likely without the pushing, gnawing, and advocating for more than hope.

Comedian Chris Rock has perhaps defined the current state of race relations when he said to whites in his audience: "If you had a chance, none of you would trade places with me—and I'm rich!" But I have witnessed some signs that Blacks may not always be victims of the past—the election of Barack Obama as president, for example. A younger generation of whites is defining decency as patriotism and intervening against the prevailing incivility of racial biases.

I am a member of the last generation that lived under legal segregation. We are victims of a conspiracy among an older generation of Blacks who were taught to comply with the humiliation from white injustice to avoid white violence. I've remained bitter from my youth to my old age. However, Obama's speech on race relations was a life-changing experience for me. This great and hopeful nation can only be united as people, if people unite against the division, be it Black or white.

Looking back, I'm still very proud I fought, awaiting the day when I can be just as proud to be an American without racial handicaps. Until then, I am still remembering that God, the architect of the universe, is good.

For now, the calm is convenient for all but those whose lives were forever disfigured by the inhumanity of the Tulsa Race Riot of 1921. Most of the survivors are now gone. May they well rest in peace.

Epilogue

SINCE THE COMPLETION of my father's memoir in 2014, Greenwood and Tulsa have changed. Both downtown Tulsa and Greenwood were thriving communities in the early 1900's only to give way to decay, vacancy and minimal commerce of the 70's, 80's and 90's. Today both Greenwood and downtown Tulsa are thriving with new construction, bike paths, and the entrepreneurial spirit of new commerce. With the passing of all the 1921 Massacre survivors, and the resurrection of the energy that surrounded Greenwood 40 years ago, it has become clear that the baton is being passed to a new generation of a curious and incredibly diverse people across not only Tulsa but the country as well.

"*Growing up Ross*" was indeed a perpetual learning experience. He wanted us to have an experience that looked and felt vastly different than that of his childhood. He introduced us to history, culture, how to treat people — (regardless of how you are treated) and importance of truth — (he would use "Jedi mind tricks" to get us to be truthful).

In conjunction with my mother, we visited a restaurant every Thursday. My parents were constantly told by the European-American patrons how well-behaved we were. My mother would always respond to them with: "Compared to what?" We very rarely ate fast food, or from canned goods. Our meals were always prepared fresh. To this day we celebrate holidays as a family, go on trips as a family, and my father still provides financial support to my mother even though they have been divorced for over 40 years.

He would teach us some amazingly simple life lessons that we still use and have passed on to our kids, such as:

When faced with a situation and you do not know want to do: DO

SOMETHING!

Be Creative!

When we were small children, one of his favorite stories he would read to us was the "The Emperor Has No Clothes". I did not ask why he always referred to this story until I began my career in corporate America.

When we would ask for the new GI Joe with the kung fu grip, he would tell us no. We would tell him "you're making us suffer." His response: "Suffering builds character."

When we sat around the fireplace as children, he overheard us wishing for a million dollars and what we do if we had it, he proceeded to tell us that was a waste of a wish (his language was a lot more colorful). Then he would drop the hammer on us with something that made our heads explode. "If you're going to wish for some money…Wish for all the money in the world! Your chances of getting it is **exactly** the same."

We all preferred spankings from my dad versus my mother. My mother never got tired. However, he never told us that this was going to hurt you more than it was going to hurt him. It was not going to hurt him at all!! If you laughed while someone was getting a spanking, then you were next.

My freshman year at Oklahoma State, as we walked around the campus, he gave me some sage advice that I have treasured to this day.

In class do two things consistently: sit on the front row and ask questions.

Let no one tell you how good or how bad you are, you already know.

Hope is not a strategy.

When dealing with difficult people/bullies; check 'em hard, check 'em early and check 'em often.

I know I speak for my siblings when I say that our childhood was awesome. We experienced different places, types of foods, and cultures. While he was the Asst Editor at the Gary Post Tribune, we watched all the parades for the roof of the Gary Port Tribune. Went to beach every day, met celebrities such as Fred Williamson, Richard

Epilogue

Roundtree, Dick Gregory ate greens at our house, Ossie Davis and Ruby Dee at Carver Stadium. We had a car when we turned 16 (it was a hooptie from my uncles' junkyard, but it was a car). We were not well-off by any stretch and barely middle-class, but he made sure we had what we needed. If his goal were to make sure that our childhood looked vastly different than his, mission accomplished. Thank you, Representative Ross!!

—*Edward Ross*

∽

LEADERSHIP COMES WITH SACRIFICE. The sacrifices he has made for his family, the community of Tulsa, Oklahoma, the African-American community, and America is and will always be honored and revered on the world's stage. His leadership and flexibility are beautifully demonstrated through his writing and his career resume. Through a relentless will, focused intentions, and the love of the people, he managed to achieve great accomplishments.

Although America's racial transformation is far from over, his influence was able to transform his community, Tulsa, and Oklahoma. These memoirs, aligned with his career, will give the reader the greatest understanding and appreciation for Representative Don Ross's legacy. As a grandson, a member of the community, and a fan — great job grandpa.

—*Antonio Ross*

∽

PILLAGE OF HOPE is a testimony to Don Ross's dedication to Black liberation.

I first met Don in 1966 when I was a Vista volunteer living in Greenwood. As a mentor and a friend for over 50 years, he has exemplified what it means to live a life dedicated to racial justice. Over that time, as we visited each other's cities and had colorful phone calls blaming each other for conservative politics in the other person's state, the bond remained strong. I knew the weight that Don carried in the political battles in Oklahoma, including his fight for restitution for the massacre, the way he worked to heal the pain of the Oklahoma City terrorist attack, and his passionate, unending fight for Greenwood and North Tulsa.

I learned from Don to be generous in honoring and giving credit to people's struggles. His attempt to win reparations and his role with Senator Maxine Horner in the construction of the Greenwood Cultural Center were among his proudest endeavors. At the center of his years of work was his determination to honor the survivors of the massacre and their families.

Visiting Don over the last two years, I had a chance to sit in the chair next to his bed as he battled illness and talk well into the night sharing stories, debating politics and celebrating his family, his children and his beloved grandchildren.

A year ago Don made sure I had the privilege to meet the amazing Senator Maxine Horner, holding a party at his house with family and community leaders.

Don has always been a uniter, not a divider. He has a deep sense of history that he has conveyed to his family, friends and followers. He has broken down walls even with some of the most conservative people in Oklahoma. And he helped uncover story by story the real toll of the 1921 massacre.

This memoir sheds light on what led to the success of Black Wall Street; the white supremacist laws and culture that nurtured the enemies of that success and exploded on May 31, 1921; the aftermath of the massacre; the resilience of the Black community; and the effort to commemorate and repair the harm.

We are all the beneficiaries of Don Ross's life.

—*Larry Miller*

Recommendations

The state of Oklahoma and city of Tulsa should:
- Implement the recommendations of the "Tulsa Race Riot Commission," made 20 years ago to the state of Oklahoma and the city of Tulsa.
- Create a mechanism to make reparations to the descendants of those harmed from the massacre in Greenwood and the events that followed efforts to rebuild. Reparations should address the impact of discrimination, structural/Institutional racism and segregation faced by African-Americans in Tulsa today.
- Introduce and pass legislation that would clear the legal hurdle of the statute of limitations that now blocks civil claims related to the massacre and its aftermath.
- Commit to abandon any statute of limitations defense in claims brought against them in connection with the massacre, so that claims can be heard on the merits.
- Increase their financial support of the work of the Greenwood Cultural Center to expand the historical recognition of Black Wall Street and the massacre in Greenwood and of Oklahoma's African-American experience.

The United States Congress should:
- Reintroduce and pass legislation to eliminate the legal hurdles posed by the statute of limitations to the assertion of civil claims related to the Tulsa race massacre and its aftermath.
- Pass H.R. 40, the Commission to Study and Develop Reparation Proposals for African-Americans Act originally proposed by my friend John Conyers Jr. in 1989.

These suggestions are only a start. Tulsa's Black community, along with other communities of color and poor whites, are in dire need of improved employment, education, housing, healthcare and more.

God bless the people of Tulsa and Oklahoma. God bless the United States of America and all the good people of this earth.

Resources

Oklahoma Commission to Study the Tulsa Race Riot 2001. Tulsa Race Riot. Commissioned by The Oklahoma State Legislature: Sponsors: Representative Don Ross (Tulsa) and Senator Maxine Horner (Tulsa)
https://21400bc3-acb9-420d-98ec-ac1476caeba6.filesusr.com/ugd/979868_5d1858b59af5426482731942624d9bae.pdf

Ross, Don. 2003. *A Century of African-American Experience. Greenwood: Ruins, Resilience and Renaissance.* Oklahoma: Greenwood Cultural Center.

Franklin, John Hope. Fall 2005. *The Two Worlds of Race: A Historical View.* Daedalus Vol. 134, No. 4, pp. 118-133. The MIT Press on behalf of American Academy of Arts & Sciences
https://www.jstor.org/stable/20028017

Teall, Kaye M., ed. 1971. *Black History in Oklahoma.* Oklahoma City, Oklahoma: Oklahoma City Public Schools.

DeWitty, Dorothy Moses 1997. *Tulsa: Tale of Two Cities.* Langston, Oklahoma: Melvin B. Tolson Black Heritage Center, Langston University.

Ellsworth, Scott 1982. *Death in a Promised Land.* Louisiana: Louisiana State University Press.

Brophy, Alfred L., 2002. *Reconstructing the Dreamland.* New York: Oxford University Press.

Madigan, Tim 2001. *The Burning.* New York: Thomas Dunne Books, St. Martin's Press.

McWhirter, Cameron 2011. *Red Summer.* New York: St. Martin's Press.

Greenwood Cultural Center
https://greenwoodculturalcenter.com/

Oklahoma Eagle
http://theoklahomaeagle.net/

Black Wall Street Times
https://tinyurl.com/yy6hf764

Oklahoma History Center Curriculum
https://tinyurl.com/y4tfl289

Digital Collection through the Oklahoma Digital Prairies available to browse: https://digitalprairie.ok.gov/digital/collection/race-riot

Rethinking schools and Zinn Education Project Curriculum:
https://www.zinnedproject.org/news/teaching-the-tulsa-massacre-99-years-later/

Traveling exhibition available through the Tulsa Historical Society, but only within the Tulsa Metro Area, but there are lesson plans available for other institutions:
https://www.tulsahistory.org/learn/programs-tours/greenwood-tulsa-race-massacre-traveling-exhibit/

Atlantic graphic depiction of Tulsa massacre
https://www.theatlantic.com/sponsored/hbo-2019/the-massacre-of-black-wall-street/3217/

PBS documentary
https://www.pbs.org/wgbh/americanexperience/films/t-town/

America's Black Holocaust Museum
https://www.abhmuseum.org/

Interviews with survivors:

Olivia Hooker.
https://tinyurl.com/y3aoqb86

Eldoris McCondiche.
https://blackoutloud.wordpress.com/2020/07/01/tulsa-ok-race-massacre-survivor-interview/
Essie Lee Johnson Beck.
https://tinyurl.com/y2hhgs35

Beulah Laure Smith, Myrtle Rollerson, Eunice Jackson, Jobie Elizabeth Holderness,E. McCondichie,Kinney Booker, Essie Lee Johnson, Juanita Arnold, and Phinnis Bell.
https://tinyurl.com/yyx42jff

Black Wallstreet videos:
https://youtu.be/hGNlcQutKRA 42 min
https://youtu.be/y0Je8sGi7Wg 1 hr 43 min
https://youtu.be/MYTIj4_Rbow 1 ½ min

www.ingramcontent.com/pod-product-compliance
Lightning Source LLC
Chambersburg PA
CBHW022043160426
43209CB00002B/52